INTRODUCTION BY DANIEL J. BOORSTIN

THE UNITED STATES
CAPITOL

PHOTOGRAPHS BY

FRED J. MAROON

TEXT BY

SUZY MAROON

STEWART, TABORI & CHANG

NEW YORK

THE UNITED STATES CAPITOL
is published in cooperation with
THE UNITED STATES CAPITOL PRESERVATION COMMISSION

The book was supported by generous grants from
EASTMAN KODAK COMPANY
THE GRAND LODGE F. & A. M. OF PENNSYLVANIA
OCEAN SPRAY CRANBERRIES

Photographs copyright © 1993 Fred J. Maroon
Text copyright © 1993 Suzy Maroon
Introduction copyright © 1993 Daniel J. Boorstin
Black-and-white illustrations on pages 36, 40, 42 (bottom), and 43 courtesy of the Architect of the Capitol. Black-and-white illustrations on pages 26, 32, and 38 courtesy of the Library of Congress.

Edited by Ann ffolliott

Published in 1993 by
Stewart, Tabori & Chang, Inc.
575 Broadway, New York,
New York 10012

Distributed in the U.S. by
Workman Publishing
708 Broadway, New York,
New York 10003

Distributed in Canada by
Canadian Manda Group
P.O. Box 920 Station U
Toronto, Ontario M8Z 5P9

Distributed in all other territories by
Melia Publishing Services
P.O. Box 1639, Maidenhead,
Berkshire SL6 6YZ, England

Central and South American accounts should contact
Export Sales Manager
Stewart, Tabori & Chang

Library of Congress
Cataloging-in-Publication Data
Maroon, Fred J., 1924–

The United States Capitol /
Fred J. Maroon ; text by
Suzy Maroon ; introduction by
Daniel J. Boorstin.

Includes bibliographical references and index.
ISBN 1-55670-316-3 —
ISBN 1-55670-319-8 (pbk.)

1. United States Capitol
(Washington, D.C.)
2. Washington (D.C.)—
Buildings, structures, etc.
I. Maroon, Suzy, 1938–
II. Boorstin, Daniel J. (Daniel
Joseph), 1914– . III. Title.
NA4413.W37M37 1993
725'.11'09753—dc20
92-35906   CIP

Printed in the United States of America

PAGE 1: EARLY MORNING LIGHT ON THE COLUMNS OF THE HOUSE WING, EAST FRONT. PAGE 2: THE BRONZE DOORS INTO THE SENATE WING, EAST FRONT, WERE DESIGNED BY THOMAS CRAWFORD AND FEATURE BATTLE SCENES FROM THE REVOLUTIONARY WAR. PAGE 3: A MEDALLION HEAD OF GEORGE WASHINGTON IN FRESCO BY CONSTANTINO BRUMIDI, IN A SUBCOMMITTEE ROOM OF THE HOUSE APPRO- PRIATIONS COMMITTEE. PAGES 6-7: A BREAK IN THE CLOUDS ILLUMINATES THE CAPITOL.

PREFACE

FRED J. MAROON

*I*N 1990, WHLE I WAS WATCHING the Fourth of July celebrations on the Mall and listening to the National Symphony Orchestra's thundering rendition of Tchaikovsky's 1812 Overture, the majestic beauty of the United States Capitol struck me in a way it never had before. Although I had lived in Washington for more than forty years, and the Capitol had been the focus of many photographic assignments, it was as if I were seeing the building for the first time. I realized I did not know as much about its architecture as I would like, and wondered what it would take to obtain permission to undertake a comprehensive photographic study of it. I was aware of the restrictions placed on photographers both in and around the Capitol; even the simple act of setting up a tripod guarantees a confrontation with one or more of the twelve hundred Capitol police who patrol the building around the clock, seven days a week. My preliminary inquiries elicited various responses, most of which could be summed up in two words: "Forget it!" But I was too intrigued by the photographic possibilities to be deterred.

The Capitol comes under the jurisdiction of not one, but three independent authorities: the Senate, the House of Representatives, and the Architect of the Capitol. However, I learned that all three authorities were represented on the United States Capitol Preservation Commission, which was at that time beginning to plan the celebrations in connection with the bicentennial of the laying of the Capitol cornerstone by George Washington in 1793. After fourteen months and many meetings, I entered into an agreement with the United States Capitol Preservation Commission; the Commission had determined "that a collection of interpretive architectural images of the Capitol, in book form, would be particularly suited to mark the occasion."

It took me more than a year to complete the bulk of the photography, ending with the inauguration of President Clinton in January 1993. Most of my work had to be done during off hours and weekends so as not to interfere with normal business when the building was open to the public or when Congress was in session.

It was the most technically challenging subject I have ever undertaken. With the exception of the Rotunda, there is little or no daylight in some of the large interior spaces, such as the Hall of Columns, the Old Supreme Court, and the Old Senate Chamber. And yet the effect I wanted to achieve was that of existing light. As simple as this sounds, it often necessitated twelve or more lights, which in turn meant two to four assistants and two to four carts of equipment. Sometimes it took two days before I was sufficiently satisfied with the quality and balance of the lights to start exposing film.

Professional photographers see many things in the course of their careers. Time spent at St. Peter's in Rome, at the Pyramids, and in Persepolis lifted me to emotional highs that the resulting photographs can still reawaken to this day. When all the lights were finally in place and calibrated to balance and harmonize properly in the Capitol, I felt that same rush of exhilaration as I looked through the viewer and finally exposed the film. I feel fortunate to be in a profession where, after forty years, it is still possible to find a subject that can get the adrenaline pumping with all the vitality one usually identifies with the Christmas mornings of one's youth.

This book reflects the architects, artists, and craftsmen who created the Capitol. It honors the generations of public servants who have taken part in the experiment of government of the people, by the people, for the people. And it is dedicated to all men and women who embrace the democratic ideals upon which this country was founded, and which the Capitol symbolizes.

CONTENTS

DANIEL J. BOORSTIN

EMOCRACIES, and especially ours in the United States, are conspicuously weak in ritual. In its place we Americans have made architecture an enduring public affirmation of community. This is not surprising, for our kind of government depends on bringing people and their representatives together. And we are fortunate to possess an elegant architectural metaphor for our political visions and hopes—our national Capitol. This year we celebrate the two hundredth anniversary of the laying of the cornerstone. The British, with whom we share the traditions of representative government, have not been nearly so fortunate. For most of the last century the Houses of Parliament have met in a building of the Gothic Revival, a picturesque but irrelevant reach for a long-past era, rebuilt after portions of it were destroyed by German bombs in World War II. But our Capitol survives from its beginning as a brilliant symbol both of the aspirations of our nation's founders and of the capacity of representative government to adapt to an expanding nation and an advancing technology.

The only ritual required by our Constitution is the President's inauguration, and the Capitol, as the traditional stage for this celebration, has become a witness and a symbol of continuity. So, too, our Capitol gives order and dignity to our political memories as a traditional dramatic setting for our repeating communal experience, the sessions of our Congress.

By contrast to ritual, architecture requires no priesthood and reminds us of the *material* foundations of community. The log cabin, the balloon-frame house, and the distinctive American hotels in our expanding West dramatized our nation's geographic and social mobility just as the skyscraper embodied triumphs of technology. Meanwhile our national Capitol has dramatized the paradox of a New World nation living by the most venerable written constitution still in use, in a building that faithfully embodies the tastes and hopes of its founders.

The government of this new nation would be centered in the first city expressly built to be a nation's capital. The city planner chosen by George Washington, the French-born Pierre Charles L'Enfant (1754–1825), had in mind a kind of new Paris of boulevards, vistas, and parks, and with the added charms of Versailles. Ironically his plan became a capital city quite unlike any of its Old World counterparts. One of his unexpected achievements was also to provide the setting for a national Capitol without precedent.

The choice of the site on the Potomac can remind us of how dramatically the dimensions of national aspirations have changed in the last two centuries. In that age of slow and cumbersome overland travel, it was assumed that the seat of government for this nation of Atlantic colonies should be an Atlantic port city. And of possible sites, a location on the Potomac River seemed at the time to offer ready access to the Ohio Valley and the adjacent West where the nation was expected to expand. This hope became a practical reality in 1784 with the organization of the Potomac Company, dedicated to boosting inland navigation. George Washington was its first president. The company aimed to raise private funds to build canals connecting the Potomac with the Ohio River. So the Potomac would be a headquarters for the young nation's expansive westward hopes. Textbook accounts, looking backward from the Civil War, emphasize the choice of the site as a sectional compromise between North and South and an omen of the conflict to come. But we must not forget that in the minds of those who made the decision and passed the "Residence Act" in 1790, the future of a westward-expanding nation loomed large. And the hopes of George Washington himself commanded respect.

It proved easier to fix the Capitol's site on Jenkins' Hill than to settle on its design. The difficulties reveal the problems and opportunities of a new transatlantic nation separated from the sources of European culture. President Washington wrote to Secretary of State Thomas Jefferson that the Capitol "ought to be upon a scale far superior to any thing in *this* Country." Only a domed building, Washington insisted, would have the required grandeur and elegance. Since there were no domed structures in the country at the time, Washington could only have seen them in illustrations. Still the Dome had already become a popular American metaphor for the Constitution—a "beauteous Dome" providing "a great Federal Superstructure," supported by the thirteen states and in turn protecting them. An enthusiastic poet, Benjamin Russell in his "Birth of Columbia" in 1788, had already imagined:

> Behold the FEDERAL DOME majestic rise!
> On lofty Pillars rear'd, whose ample base,
> On firm foundation laid, unmov'd shall stand,
> 'Till happy your unnumbered circles run,
> The TEMPLE OF CELESTIAL LIBERTY!

While warning against "extravagance" in public buildings, the prudent Washington wanted "a chaste plan sufficiently capacious and convenient for a period not *too* remote, but one to which we may *reasonably* look forward." Some sixteen entries in the architectural competition for the Capitol have survived, but none could satisfy these hopes.

The versatile Thomas Jefferson took an active interest. He had been designing his own home at Monticello, and had recently designed the Capitol of Virginia on the model of a classic temple; Jefferson now urged a similar design on one of the competitors, Stephen Hallet, a French architect living in Philadelphia. But Hallet could not adapt Jefferson's Virginia design to the larger scale of a national capitol. Jefferson then suggested a spherical model, of which the Pantheon in Rome seemed the most perfect example and the Panthéon in Paris seemed the most suitable to the American site. Jefferson himself made some sketches, but Hallet could not translate them into a suitable plan for the building. Still, the basic scheme—a central dome with wings—would become the style of American state capitols.

The outcome of the competition for the design of the Capitol was symbolic. The winner was no architect of distinction but an amateur—the thirty-three-year-old William Thornton (1759–1828), born in a community of the Society of Friends in one of the Virgin Islands. He had been trained as a physician in Scottish universities, but had never practiced medicine. He had become an American citizen in 1788, had lived in Philadelphia, and had designed a new building for the Library Company there. Thornton recalled how, with the rashness of the amateur, he had made his first-prize-winning design. "When I travelled, I never thought of architecture. But I got some books and worked a few days, then gave a plan in the ancient Ionic order, which carried the day." He had already proven his inventive imagination when in 1778 he had begun collaborating with John Fitch in his pioneer design for steamboats operated by paddles. Fitch's third boat, named the *Thornton,* reaching a speed of eight miles an hour had made the regular packet run on the Delaware River until it was retired in 1790.

Thornton's versatility was astonishing. His skills as a draftsman and artist helped persuade people to adopt his architectural plans. He won a medal from the American Philosophical Society for his treatise on the elements of written language, and he left three unpublished novels. He wrote a pioneer work on teaching the deaf and was active in antislavery movements. He also tried to found a national university in Washington. Among his grander visions was a union of the two American continents, with a capital near Panama and a canal uniting the two oceans.

The first grandiose project to incite Thornton's imagination was the design for the new United States Capitol. When he heard of the competition, he wrote the Commissioners offering to bring them his plan. Arriving in Washington, after a glimpse of Hallet's efforts to embody Jefferson's themes, he produced a new version. When President Washington voiced enthusiasm for the "grandeur, simplicity and convenience" of Thornton's still unfinished plan, this ensured its adoption. Jefferson praised Thornton's plan as "simple, noble, beautiful, excellently distributed, and moderate in size." But since Thornton was neither a professional architect nor a builder, Hallet was engaged to supervise the construction. On September 18, 1793, the cornerstone was laid by Washington himself. Jefferson, whose architectural ideas would be embodied in the building, but who had no taste for ceremony, was not present.

"Thornton's plan," an emphatically collaborative product, provided the basic features that survived the two following centuries. This was a central dome facing east and west, flanked by two balanced wings extending north and south. The simple essential concept remarkably weathered the changing views of several architects, lack of funds, perils of fire, wartime shortages and destruction, and it proved capable of expansion to meet the needs of a vastly larger nation.

The architects engaged on the Capitol during these two centuries are a rough epitome of American architectural history before the skyscraper. Jefferson engaged the architect-engineer Benjamin H. Latrobe (1764–1820), a leader of the Greek Revival who had assisted him with detail on the Capitol in Richmond, to build the South wing and to rebuild after the whole building had been left "a most magnificent ruin" from fires set by British troops on August 24, 1814. After Latrobe's departure in 1817, President Monroe hired Charles Bulfinch (1763–1844). Often called the first American professional architect, Bulfinch was already noted for his design of the Massachusetts State House in Boston. During his years as Architect of the Capitol (1817–1830) Bulfinch designed the Rotunda, improved and redesigned many details, and finished the construction with the East Portico in 1826.

The expansion of the nation meant that by 1850, the Capitol needed more space. After a competition produced no clear winner, President Millard Fillmore appointed a fellow Whig, Thomas U. Walter (1811–1876) of Philadelphia, to design the extension. Walter, son of a bricklayer and himself a master bricklayer, had engineering experience and had trained under William Strickland (1788–1854), a master of the Greek Revival style. During his years as Architect of the Capitol (1851–1865), Walter expanded and rebuilt much of the building to its present form. Drawing on the suggestions of others, his extension of the Capitol took the form of two large wings at right angles to the existing building and connected to the north and south ends of the existing building by narrow corridors. These extensions too were thoroughly in the classical tradition of the original structure. The ritual

symbolism of the Capitol was flamboyantly declaimed by Daniel Webster in a two-hour-long oration at the laying of the cornerstone of the extensions on July 4, 1851. The new wings joined to the old stood for the new states (Texas and California) and the promise of still more to come—proclaiming that the Union, like the Capitol, "may endure for ever!" Ironically it was President Franklin Pierce's able Secretary of War, Jefferson Davis, who as senator had helped secure the first appropriations for the extensions and now directed the work. Through Montgomery C. Meigs, a strong-minded captain in the Corps of Engineers, Davis took an intimate interest in the new construction, commissioning works of art and trying to increase the elegance of the interior.

A spark from a stove on Christmas Eve, 1851, which set off a fire that gutted the Library of Congress in the West Central building, would, surprisingly, put this grand Greek Revival Capitol in the vanguard of American technology. When Walter rebuilt the Library in the Capitol he constructed the first room in America of fireproof cast iron. There the Library remained until its removal across the street to its elegant neo-Renaissance building in 1897. The Library fire would decisively affect the grand silhouette and future shape of the Capitol, for it aroused fears that a fire igniting Bulfinch's wooden dome might engulf the whole building. Walter seized the opportunity to replace, elevate, and modernize Bulfinch's dome. The extensions of the Capitol had dwarfed Bulfinch's dome, and besides offering a fire-hazard the old dome leaked.

For Walter's radical innovation—a double dome—there was European precedent in the Panthéon in Paris. Assisted by modern American industrial technology, the bold Walter saw that a double dome could solve several problems at once. His concept was an inner dome of stone within a frame of cast iron that would be covered on the outside by stone masonry in the neoclassical style. So he imagined a high dome of unprecedented grandeur and elegance.

It was cast iron, surprisingly, that finally would make this inspiring stone monument possible. The old foundation of Bulfinch's Rotunda could not have supported the weight of a high dome of solid stone. But the newly developed cast iron provided a much lighter frame for a dome soaring above the old one. Some in Congress and the architectural profession were skeptical or outraged—at displacing the hallowed stones of Greece and Rome by a vulgar industrial material. A congressman from Maryland objected on the floor of the House that while iron might make "a good dome," still nowhere did "the history of the architecture of the world present an example of an iron dome." But the newly formed American Institute of Architects heard a characteristically American defense: "It is obviously not proper or just to reject contemptuously new building materials and new constructive devices, because they were unknown to Phidias, to Palladio or William of Wyckham . . . The cheapness of iron, its rapidity and ease of workmanship . . . in the present state of society render that metal especially precious as a means of popular architecture."

The Congress not only approved the iron dome but was impatient for its completion. Members were persuaded by the economy and the speed with which an iron dome could be built. Here was the opportunity, too, in a "season of universal depression in the iron trade" to provide "grateful relief to a large number of necessitous but worthy and industrious men." The new iron dome incorporated some 9 million pounds of cast iron, most of it cast in Brooklyn, New York, at a cost of $1,047,291.

Despite Civil War shortages of men and materials, the fifth and final section of the bronze crowning statue of Freedom (19 feet 7 inches tall) by Thomas Crawford was put in place on December 2, 1863. When Crawford first submitted his design for Freedom to Secretary of War Jefferson Davis in 1856, Davis requested a figure "much more vigorous," which was duly supplied. Davis also objected to the figure's headdress—a "liberty cap" which he found "inappropriate to a people who were born free and would not be enslaved . . . its use, as the badge of the freed slave." Crawford obligingly replaced the liberty cap with "a Helmet, the crest . . . composed of an eagle's head and a bold arrangement of feathers suggested by the costume of our Indian tribes." With a strict order against speech-making, this statue of an armed Freedom triumphant in war and peace was dedicated by a thirty-five-gun salute. The dome was finished when Constantino Brumidi completed his *The Apotheosis of Washington* in December 1865. On the Capitol grounds we can still enjoy the work of the greatest American landscape architect, Frederick Law Olmsted (1822–1903), who made the grounds into a public park and embellished the setting of the Capitol with the marble terrace to the west (1886–1891) and so provided a splendid site for inaugurations.

When Walter retired in 1865 his place was taken by his assistant Edward Clark (Architect of the Capitol, 1865–1902), whose main achievement was to modernize the facilities, gradually introducing electric light in place of gas in the 1880s. But before gaslight was removed, a gas explosion in the North Wing dramatized the need to replace all remaining wooden ceilings with cast steel. The Architects after Clark—Elliott Woods (1902–1923) and David Lynn (1923–1954)—were devoted mainly to refurbishing the interior, enlarging facilities, and providing underground parking. The exterior shape of the building was modified when the East Front was extended by 32 feet to provide aesthetic balance for the soaring dome, incidentally adding some ninety rooms. George M. White (1971–   ), as Architect of the Capitol, has taken steps to keep pace with the latest technology, including electronic voting and television coverage of House and Senate debates. The historic role of the Capitol was dramatized by the Bicentennial celebration in 1976 by restoration of the Old Senate Chamber and the Old Supreme Court Chamber. Continuing exhibits of documents and improved interpreting services have awakened visitors to the significance of the building. The deteriorating West Central Front was restored by replacing its sandstone walls and reinforcing the structure with stainless steel rods.

Our nation's Capitol expresses in some surprising ways the remarkable capacity of our New World nation to incorporate modern technology while preserving our inheritance of the best in Western culture. The capacity of the original design to be extended happily paralleled the capacity of the Federal Union to be enlarged and of the Constitution to be amended. The hope of the framers of the Constitution for a New Nation, fulfilling and exceeding Old World expectations, was expressed by Jefferson himself. In difficult times, even before there was a grand rotunda uniting the House and Senate wings, Jefferson envisaged "the first temple dedicated to the sovereignty of the people, embellishing with Athenian taste the course of a nation looking far beyond the range of Athenian destinies." &

*T*HE CAPITOL DURING THE
BLIZZARD OF 1966. *PAGES 12-13:*
THE CAPITOL FROM THE EAST,
AT NIGHT. *PAGES 14-15:* THE
HALL OF COLUMNS, ON THE
GROUND FLOOR OF THE HOUSE
WING. *PAGES 18-19:* THE SOUTH
PORTICO OF THE HOUSE WING
AFTER SUNSET. *PAGES 20-21:*
CHERRY BLOSSOMS ON THE
WEST LAWN OF THE CAPI-
TOL GROUNDS.

BUILDING

THE

CAPITOL

AMONG the majestic build- ings and recognized land- marks of the world, it would be hard to find one that had a less auspicious beginning than the United States Capitol. A competition was held for its design, and the winning entry was the work of an amateur who sent in his design months after the competition's deadline had passed. No funds were appropriated for construction. It was to be built in a city that did not exist. And finally, in a well-intended but injudicious attempt to mollify him, the disappointed and jealous runner-up in the competition was put in charge of the construction of his rival's building. That the Capitol was built at all is testimony to the faith the Founding Fathers had in their fledgling experiment in democracy, and their determination to see the young country survive. That it has elegance and grandeur is due in large part to the sophisticated taste of Thomas Jefferson and George Washington, and to the succession of architects who would add their mark to what Jefferson described as "the first temple dedicated to the sovereignty of the people." ⟳ In many ways the Capitol is a fitting symbol of the history of the United States. The expansion of the building has paralleled the growth of the nation, from its tentative and idealistic beginnings

A PORTRAIT OF GEORGE WASHINGTON BY GILBERT STUART IN THE PRIVATE OFFICE OF THE SENATE DEMOCRATIC LEADER. *FACING PAGE:* THE TOWERING CORINTHIAN COLUMNS OF THE NEW SENATE WING.

two hundred years ago to its dominant presence today. As states were added to the Union, the need for more space in the Capitol increased. When what was then known as the "Congress House" was being designed there were thirty senators and sixty-nine representatives, whose offices consisted of the desks at which they sat. Today there are one hundred senators and 435 representatives, each of whom needs a staff able to deal with myriad issues, many of which would have been unimaginable two hundred years ago.

In 1790, the second session of the First Congress passed the "Residence Act" authorizing a permanent seat for the federal government. Nearly ten years of heated contest had preceded this, with more than thirty cities, stretching from Newburgh, New York, to Norfolk, Virginia, lobbying strenuously for the honor. Eagerness to win the prize probably was rooted less in patriotic fervor than in the expectation of the jobs and contracts that proximity to the government would bring. Furthermore, where Congress went, good roads and military defenses were bound to follow. The consensus in Congress was that the capital should be "central," but an immediate problem arose in trying to define what that meant. The geographic center of the thirteen states was, approximately, the Potomac River, but this was considerably farther south than the center of population. Northerners naturally favored the latter, arguing that citizens of a democracy need to be within striking distance of their government. Southerners countered with the contention that, for military and commercial reasons, the capital should be as geographically central as possible. The largely agricultural South was also fearful of being dominated by the more commercially oriented North. In the end, the location of the capital was a compromise between Alexander Hamilton of New York and Thomas Jefferson of Virginia. Hamilton had proposed that the federal government assume the debts incurred by the states during the Revolution—a scheme not viewed favorably in states such as Virginia whose debts had already been paid and whose citizens would therefore be taxed again for the federal debt. In a carefully orchestrated compromise, Jefferson gave his support to debt assumption—and the South got the capital.

The Residence Act stated that "a territory not exceeding ten miles square, to be located as hereafter directed on the river Potomac, at some place between the mouths of the Eastern Branch and Conococheague, be, and the same is hereby, accepted for the permanent seat of the Government of the United States." The Eastern Branch was the Anacostia River, and the mouth of the Conococheague was in Williamsport, Maryland, which meant there was a shoreline of some 105 miles from which to choose. The exact location for the city was to be selected by the three commissioners whom George Washington was to appoint to oversee construction of the city. Washington himself had obvious emotional and financial reasons for wanting the capital to be located near his beloved Mount Vernon, but he was far too principled to lobby actively for it. He held that a person in his position must "have it in his power to demonstrate the disinterestedness of his words and actions at all times, and upon all occasions." Such was the reverence in which he was held, however, that few were surprised, and even fewer annoyed, when the commissioners—Thomas Johnson, Daniel Carroll, and David Stuart—decided upon that section of the Potomac closest to Mount Vernon.

Even before the Residence Act had been passed, George Washington had received a letter from Major Pierre Charles L'Enfant, asking permission to design "the capital of this vast Empire." L'Enfant was a French military engineer who had served as a volunteer in the American Revolutionary Army and had attracted Washington's attention with his designs for fortifications. He had also received general approbation for his remodeling of New York's City Hall into Federal Hall—the first home of Congress after the Constitution was adopted and the scene of Washington's inauguration. L'Enfant grasped that here was a singular opportunity: the capital of what was destined to become one of the world's great nations was to be planned, designed, and built from scratch. Even if the means to complete the undertaking were not immediately at hand, L'Enfant knew that the decisions made at the beginning would determine the outcome, and he wanted to be the one to make those decisions. Although he lacked experience in city planning, his childhood had been spent in Versailles, where his father was a court painter, and in Paris. He knew the requirements of a beautifully laid-out city. His genius, coupled with his idealism and long-range vision, had powerful appeal to Washington. The job of planning the city was his for the asking.

The Residence Act also directed the commissioners to provide, prior to the first Monday in December 1800, "suitable buildings for the accommodation of Congress and of the President and for the public offices of the Government of the United States." In June 1791, L'Enfant and Washington conducted a survey of the area, which consisted mainly of tobacco farms, cornfields, orchards, and woods. Together they rode up what was then known as Jenkins Hill and immediately recognized it as the perfect location for the future home of Congress; in L'Enfant's words, it was "a pedestal waiting for a monument." Moreover, it was a monument *he* wanted to create. When he learned that Thomas Jefferson favored a competition to select the design for the Capitol, L'Enfant hurriedly paid a visit to George Washington at Mount Vernon to secure the honor for himself.

The President acquiesced, but stipulated that L'Enfant must cooperate with the three commissioners, a condition that proved to be L'Enfant's undoing. His plan for Washington, with its grid of alphabetical and numerical streets intersected by broad radiating avenues, creating circles and grand vistas, has been called by architectural historian Mark Girouard "arguably the most brilliant town plan ever conceived." But in executing it, L'Enfant was on a collision course not only with the pragmatism of the commissioners, but also frequently with their powerful, land-owning friends. Funds for the construction of the city's public buildings were to be raised by auctioning off lots, but L'Enfant refused to produce his plan prior to the auction for fear that speculators would begin building in ways that would interfere with his grand design. As a result, the auctions brought in far less

than the commissioners had hoped, and for this they blamed L'Enfant. His stock with the commissioners sank even lower when, in one particularly injudicious move, he ordered a house belonging to a nephew of one of them to be pulled down. Daniel Carroll of Duddington owned all of the land on which the Capitol was to be built, and he was building an addition to his house on land that he knew L'Enfant wanted for a street. L'Enfant, whose eye was ever on "the main object," threatened to raze the building. Carroll obtained an injunction, but L'Enfant ignored it and sent his men to demolish the offending addition. Carroll was outraged and L'Enfant, unrepentant: "The building of Mr. Carroll of Duddington was erected in contrariety to the plan adopted and throwing it down was doing justice to all individuals concerned."

George Washington, recognizing L'Enfant's genius and the impossibility of finding another like him in the young country, did everything in his power to persuade his headstrong protégé to cooperate with the commissioners. L'Enfant, however, complained of their "unwearied efforts . . . to cause some alterations in the plan . . . which evinces in them a greater concern to favor individual interest, than attention to secure the public good." They were looking after their friends, while he was trying to "change a wilderness into a city." He went so far as to accuse them of stirring up "mutiny among the people" and issued an ultimatum: either he be placed outside the authority of the commissioners, or they be dismissed. It was an uneven contest between a visionary and the establishment, and the commissioners won easily. L'Enfant was informed that his services were no longer required and was offered 500 guineas for his past work, which he characteristically rejected with scorn. He would have nothing further to do with planning the city. Ten years later, impoverished, he would send a pathetic request to Jefferson for some belated compensation, insisting that if he in any way deserved reproach, it was because he had

*I*N THE PRESIDENT'S ROOM CONSTANTINO BRUMIDI PAINTED THE MEMBERS OF GEORGE WASHINGTON'S FIRST CABINET. TWO OF THEM, THOMAS JEFFERSON AND ALEXANDER HAMILTON, PLAYED MAJOR ROLES IN SELECTING THE SITE OF THE FUTURE CAPITAL.

been "more faithfull to principle than ambitions—too zealous in [his] pursuits." The request was unavailing, and L'Enfant died a pauper and a forgotten man. But history is a fair judge of genius. Today L'Enfant lies buried in Arlington Cemetery, overlooking the city for which he had such hopes. Carved into his tomb is the plan he tried so hard to protect.

Whether L'Enfant had given much thought to the design of the public buildings before his dismissal is uncertain. He claimed to be carrying ideas around in his head, but no plans had been produced. He had, however, fixed the site of the future "Congress House". It was to sit atop Jenkins Hill, at the intersection of twelve broad avenues, visible from afar and affording a dramatic vista from all directions. On March 14, 1792, shortly after L'Enfant's dismissal, the commissioners did what Jeffer-

It is tempting to wonder whether Jefferson had a secret motive in urging such a competition. He did submit an anonymous entry of his own to the White House competition, under the initials "A.Z.," but it won no prize. What is certain is that he was highly knowledgeable and opinionated about architecture. He was an ardent admirer of Palladio and of early Roman architecture, and he believed that the Capitol should imitate "one of the models of antiquity which have had the approbation of thousands of years." Washington, for his part, knew little about architecture, but was a man of good taste. Both he and Jefferson, like other educated men of their day, were well versed in the political ideas of Athens and Rome, and wanted the capital of the new republic to reflect the values it had inherited from them.

By the deadline, at least sixteen designs for the Capitol

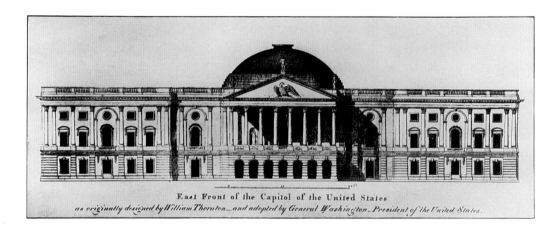

East Front of the Capitol of the United States
as originally designed by William Thornton—and adopted by General Washington—President of the United States.

ℰAST ELEVATION OF THE REVISED DESIGN FOR THE CAPITOL BY WILLIAM THORNTON, CA. 1796. THE CENTRAL PART IS DERIVED FROM THE PANTHEON IN ROME; THE WINGS SUGGEST ENGLISH COUNTRY HOUSES OF THE EIGHTEENTH CENTURY. (*LIBRARY OF CONGRESS*)

son had recommended earlier and placed the following announcement in the major newspapers:

A PREMIUM

of a lot in the city, to be designated by impartial judges, and $500, or a medal of that value, at the option of the party, will be given by the Commissioners of Federal Buildings to persons who, before the 15th day of July, 1792, shall produce them the most approved plan, if adopted by them, for a Capitol to be erected in the city, and $250 or a medal for the plan deemed next in merit to the one they shall adopt; . . .

The specifications for the building called for a room for senators and a room for representatives, each with a lobby or antechamber, a conference room able to accommodate three hundred people, and twelve rooms for committees and clerks.

had been submitted. The best of them was inadequate, the worst of them ludicrous. There were few trained architects in the country at that time; most buildings, even courthouses and statehouses, were designed and built by master masons or master carpenters. Nothing of the magnitude of the Capitol had ever been attempted. The least offensive design was the work of Stephen Hallet, an able French architect who had fled to America during the French Revolution. His plan, which had wings on either side of a central dome, was considered by Jefferson to be good enough so that, with extensive modifications, something acceptable could be made of it. The commissioners invited Hallet to Washington to work with them on revisions, and he, not unreasonably, considered himself to be the de facto winner of the competition.

It was not to be that simple. Four months after the official close of the competition a letter was received from

Dr. William Thornton, seeking permission to submit a late entry. Thornton was a physician who lived on Tortola in the British Virgin Islands. He had been born in 1759 in a British Quaker colony on Jost Van Dyke, a nearby island, and had been educated in England and Scotland. Knowledgeable, discriminating, and entertaining, he was a man of unusually broad interests, including painting, poetry, philosophy, astronomy, horse breeding, steamboats, government, and architecture. On learning of the Capitol competition, he spent a few minutes regretting that he had not studied architecture, and then set about rectifying that omission by studying night and day for weeks before submitting his design in January 1793.

Thornton had done his homework carefully. He knew that Jefferson's approval of any design was crucial, and he knew how much Jefferson esteemed Palladio and early Roman architecture. The design Thornton produced had two wings, for the Senate and House of Representatives, flanking a central section with a portico in front and a dome directly inspired by the Pantheon in Rome. It met with instant and unconditional approval from Jefferson: "Thornton's plan had captivated the eyes and the judgment of all. It is simple, noble, beautiful, excellently arranged, and moderate in size. . . . Among its admirers none are more decided than he whose decision is most important." He was referring, of course, to George Washington, who had this to say about the plan: "Grandeur, simplicity, and convenience appear to be so well combined in this plan of Dr. Thornton's. . . ."

Thornton was awarded the prize on April 5, 1793. Not forgotten, however, was Stephen Hallet, who had continued to work on his own design, confident that the prize was his. In an effort to assuage his disappointment, the commissioners voted to give him an equal monetary prize. Then, in what amounted to an unwitting act of sabotage, they asked Hallet to look over Thornton's plans and estimate of costs, and appointed him superintendent of the construction of his rival's building.

On August 1, 1793, the first foundations of the building were laid, using the cheap, easy, and not very sound "continental trench" method. The city commissioners were businessmen, not architects, and usually awarded contracts to the lowest bidder. The continental trench entailed digging a trench, throwing stones or rubble into it, and dumping mortar over the top. It also en-

A PAINTING ON THE EAST CORRIDOR CEILING, FIRST FLOOR OF THE HOUSE WING, DEPICTS GEORGE WASHINGTON LAYING THE CAPITOL CORNERSTONE ON SEPTEMBER 18, 1793. THE PAINTER IS ALLYN COX, WHO DECORATED THE HOUSE CORRIDORS BETWEEN 1973 AND 1982.

tailed, more often than not, redoing the whole thing properly not too long afterward, and the Capitol was no exception. Parts of the building were already falling into disrepair by the time Congress moved into it in 1800, and the foundations would have to be largely rebuilt. On September 18, 1793, the cornerstone of the building was laid by George Washington in an elaborate Masonic ceremony. Accompanied by members of the Alexandria Volunteer Artillery and local Masonic lodges, the President led the procession from "President's Square" next to the White House up Capitol Hill, not along anything remotely like the grand parade route that exists as Pennsylvania Avenue today, but over terrain so rough that at one point the procession had to cross a creek on a log. According to newspaper reports of the day, the President wore a Masonic apron said to have been made for him by the wife of General Lafayette. With the cornerstone he placed a large engraved silver plate, ". . . on which were deposited corn, wine and oil, when the whole congregation joined in reverential prayer, which was succeeded by Masonic chanting honors and volley from the artillery." There followed an oration by the Grand Master, pro tempore, after which the "whole company retired to an extensive booth where an ox of 500 pounds' weight was barbecued, of which the company generally partook, with every abundance of other recreation. The festival concluded with fifteen successive volleys from the artillery, whose military discipline and manoeuvres merit every commendation. Before dark

the whole company departed with joyful hopes of the production of their labor."

The exact location of the cornerstone remains a mystery, despite repeated attempts to locate it. It is known to be in the "southeast corner," but whether that refers to the Senate (north) or House (south) wing is uncertain. A concerted effort to find it was made in 1958 when much of the old foundation was exposed prior to extending the East Front. As of now the search continues.

To be fair, there were certain elements of Thornton's design that needed revision, and Hallet lost no time in identifying all of them—and more. He pointed to rooms without windows, staircases with inadequate headroom, and columns that obstructed the view in the large conference room. And he criticized the design for its size and cost. Thornton had wanted the exterior of the building, as well as the main parts of the interior, to be marble, and he would have preferred Italian marble at that. He also liked mahogany, and he protested any decrease in the size of the building. (In this last he was prophetic; less than twenty years after its completion the building had been outgrown.) As for his marble exterior, it was simply beyond the means of the young country, and it would fall to later architects in more prosperous times to realize what Thornton could not.

Hallet, in charge of construction, was ideally situated to make on-the-job changes to Thornton's design—a task he approached with relish. Increasingly he saw his job as not so much to revise Thornton's plan as to develop his own. However, in radically changing the foundations for the central section from the rotunda Thornton had designed to his own square, open courtyard, he went too far. Reprimanded by the commissioners and ordered to adhere to Thornton's original plan, Hallet resigned in 1794. He was replaced as superintendent by George Hadfield, a young English architect who was highly recommended for the job by the artist John Trumbull, then serving as secretary to the American ambassador in London.

What Hadfield found on his arrival in 1795 was a building that had progressed no higher than the foundation, and walls that were in part so poorly constructed that they had to be taken down. The plans he inherited were largely Thornton's exteriors and Hallet's interiors, and it all added up to an irresistible opportunity for Hadfield to start putting his own imprint on the Capitol. In no

One of four stained glass seals produced by the J. and G. H. Gibson Company of Philadelphia and installed when the extensions were added. This one is situated between the Senate Democratic Leader's Office and the Grand Staircase West. *Facing page:* a staircase built by Benjamin Latrobe after the fire of 1814, leading from the vestibule outside the Old Supreme Court Chamber to the Small Senate Rotunda.

time, he too was at odds with Thornton, who still wished his building to be built substantially as he had first designed it. Moreover, Hadfield's undiplomatic manner and lack of efficiency did not endear him to the commissioners. By 1798 he was gone, and James Hoban, the genial Irishman who had won the competition to design the White House, was put in charge of supervising the construction of both buildings. Compared with the Capitol, work on the White House under Hoban's direction had been relatively efficient and uncomplicated. He was a man who would not attempt to put his stamp on the building, but would get the job done.

Progress up to this point had been painfully slow. Money was a continuing problem because sales of lots in the District had failed to produce the expected revenues. Loans were difficult to obtain because the only security that could be offered was city lots, and rumors persisted that the capital might be moved to another city. In 1797 a syndicate that was purchasing land in the city—and which included Robert Morris, the wealthiest man in America at the time—went bankrupt, further dampening enthusiasm for the city as a place in which to invest. It was proving difficult to find many of the building materials needed, and in the quantities required. No building of such magnitude had ever been undertaken in the region before. There was no American glassmaker capable of producing enough glass, and shipping from England incurred long delays and inevitable breakage. There was a good stone quarry south of Washington at Aquia Creek, but insufficient manpower to quarry what was needed. Indeed, such was the shortage of skilled laborers that Jefferson advocated importing "Germans and Highlanders" to do the work, but an advertisement placed in Scotland for one hundred men failed to attract a single one. Unskilled workers were easier to find because owners were willing to hire out their slaves.

With so many problems attending the building of the Capitol, it was obvious by 1795 that the mandate to provide suitable accommodations for Congress by 1800 would be difficult, if not impossible, to meet. It was decided to concentrate all available money and men on the Senate wing, and have at least that ready by 1800.

Elsewhere in the city progress was agonizingly slow, too. Scathing comparisons were made with the city of St. Petersburg, which Peter the Great, the "Autocrat of Russia," had succeeded in finishing in nine years. By 1797, not a single house had been built on Pennsylvania Avenue, the main street connecting the Capitol and the White House. There was little sense of a city at all. There were several small clusters of houses, but so few were being built that a regulation, insisted upon by Jefferson, that all new houses built in the city be made of brick or stone had to be temporarily suspended. Workers simply could not afford such houses; most of them lived in temporary "barracks" erected near the buildings on which they worked. Washington himself contracted to have two houses built two blocks north of the Capitol. He thought they would be a good investment, since there would be a need for convenient housing once Congress moved in. But, equally important, he hoped by building to encourage others to follow suit.

Another impediment to the growth of the city was uncertainty as to the direction in which it would grow. Some, and L'Enfant was probably among them, expected the commercial section of the city to grow between the Capitol and the Eastern Branch, where the docks and wharves would be. Others predicted that the city would develop toward the west, since the White House and Georgetown were in that direction. The declining importance of water transportation eventually settled the question in favor of westward growth, but the rivalry was intense at times, and it had the effect of undermining the confidence of potential investors. Indeed, one of the few positive things that could be said in favor of Washington at that time was that it had escaped the epidemics of yellow fever that periodically gripped other East Coast cities. Its promoters were quick to give credit to the city's healthy climate and good air, overlooking the more likely explanation that it was because so few people lived there.

By 1799, however, with the deadline for finishing the Senate wing fast approaching, work on the Capitol was progressing apace, and preparations were under way to move the government from Philadelphia the following summer. But one man was not to see the culmination of the enterprise to which he had devoted so much of his hopes and energies. On December 14, 1799, George Washington died. He was buried at Mount Vernon, in accordance with his own expressed wishes, but nine days after his death Congress passed a resolution calling for him to be reburied in the Capitol. His tomb was to be in the exact center of the central section, on the subbasement level. Directly overhead, in what is now the Crypt, would stand a marble monument to him, and above that, in the Rotunda, a circular hole was to be left in the floor, permitting visitors to gaze down on the monument. It would be thirty years before the central part of the building was completed and thought could be given to implementing the resolution. By then, however, Virginia was unwilling to relinquish her treasured son, and Washington's nephew also was opposed to the idea. The state General Assembly "earnestly requested that the proprietor of Mount Vernon . . . not consent to the removal." Today the tomb in the basement is empty except for the black-draped catafalque that stands ready to bear the remains of those who lie in state in the Capitol Rotunda.

A grand procession was planned to celebrate the arrival of Congress in 1800, but an early snowfall and bickering as to who should lead the parade caused it to be canceled. In any case, only fifteen of the thirty-two senators were on hand—not enough for a quorum—and a new date for convening Congress had to be set. On November 22, with vice president Jefferson presiding, President Adams opened the second session of the Sixth Congress in its new home. In his address he said: "I congratulate the people of the United States on the assembling of

Congress at the permanent seat of their government, and I congratulate you gentlemen on the prospect of a residence not to be changed." Continuing, he prayed: "In this city may that piety and virtue, that wisdom and magnanimity, that constancy and self-government, which adorned the great character whose name it bears, be forever held in veneration!" The Senate replied: ". . . great indeed would have been our gratification if his sum of earthly happiness had been completed by seeing the Government thus peaceably convened at this place."

Such positive sentiments were harder to find in other parts of the city. The Capitol was being referred to as a "palace in the wilderness." Pennsylvania Avenue, known by the unflattering sobriquet of "the great Serbonian Bog," was little more than a muddy track, so overgrown with elder bushes that it was difficult even for pedestrians. The White House had been built, but there were few other buildings. A census taken at the time counted 109 brick and 263 wooden houses. There were several boardinghouses or "messes" near the Capitol where congressmen lived, usually two to a room. The Speaker of the House got a room to himself, and Jefferson, as vice president, was entitled to the luxury of a sitting room.

But in general such accommodations as existed were uncomfortable and expensive. Those who could afford to took lodgings in Georgetown, about three miles away from the Capitol. Hardly any brought their families with them. The few shops that existed had low inventories and high prices. New York senator Gouverneur Morris sized up the new city thus: "We want nothing here but houses, cellars, kitchens, well-informed men, amiable women, and other trifles of this kind to make our city perfect. . . . In short, it is the very best city in the world for a future residence."

By establishing Congress in its permanent home, however, the main objective had been achieved. Sharing the Senate's wing for the next few years would be the House of Representatives, the Supreme Court, the Library of Congress (founded in 1800 with an appropriation of $5,000), and the Circuit Court of the District of Columbia. The

Senate's chamber was where the Old Supreme Court Chamber is today. The first inauguration of a President in the new capital was held there on March 4, 1801, when Jefferson walked over from his boardinghouse nearby to take the oath. The House met in a room on the west side of the building, which would later contain the Library of Congress. It was hopelessly inadequate in size, and since completion of the House wing was still years away, an inexpensive temporary meeting room was hastily constructed on the foundations of the House wing and connected to the Senate wing by a covered wooden walk-

to America after the death of his wife and had attracted attention by designing the first Greek Revival building in the country, the Bank of Pennsylvania in Philadelphia. Latrobe was sharp-tongued and critical, and much of what he found awaiting him at the Capitol did not meet with his approval. He considered most of the workmanship in the Senate wing to be downright shoddy, and he also found fault with Thornton's original design. Jefferson rather artlessly urged him to meet with Thornton to discuss the elements that bothered him—a meeting that guaranteed bad blood between the two proud men from

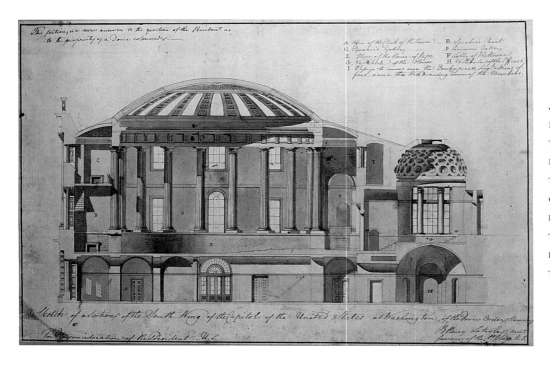

*A*N EARLY DESIGN (1804) FOR BENJAMIN LATROBE'S HALL OF THE HOUSE. ONLY THE SMALL ROTUNDA AT RIGHT SURVIVED THE FIRE OF 1814. (*LIBRARY OF CONGRESS*) *FACING PAGE:* LOOKING UP INTO THE DOME OF THE SMALL SENATE ROTUNDA FROM THE GROUND FLOOR OF THE CAPITOL.

way. Because of its shape, the room came to be known as "The Oven"; it was never a comfortable room, and when it had to be demolished so that work on the House wing could continue, the congressmen were only too happy to return to their cramped quarters in the Senate wing.

In 1794 George Washington had appointed Thornton a commissioner of the District of Columbia, and in that role Thornton had maintained an active involvement in the progress of his building. When the commission was abolished in 1802, Thornton was put in charge of the Patent Office, a job that suited him well. He had no official responsibility for the Capitol after that.

In 1803 Jefferson appointed Benjamin Henry Latrobe Surveyor of Public Buildings. Latrobe claimed to be the first professional architect to practice in America. Highly regarded in his native England, he had emigrated

then on. His relations with his patron were often difficult, too. Jefferson's involvement in the building of the Capitol fell somewhere between suggestion and command. Although always willing to listen to the "experts," there were points that he refused to concede. He wanted skylights installed in the ceiling of the House Chamber, but Latrobe knew they would cause problems with condensation and leaking. When Jefferson learned that Latrobe planned to proceed in his own way, he simply ordered that work be stopped until the skylights (which later leaked!) could be obtained. Latrobe also had to contend with Congress, and he was constantly bedeviled by the slowness and stinginess with which money was appropriated for the work. It made it hard for him to keep workmen; as funds ran out, they moved away or found other jobs, and when money again became available, the

ANOTHER OF PAINTER ALLYN COX'S MURALS IN THE CEILING OF A HOUSE CORRIDOR SHOWS THE WEST SIDE OF THE CAPITOL AS IT WAS BEING BURNED BY THE BRITISH IN 1814.

workers were not. Also, only stone, bricks, and sand could be had locally; other building materials, such as lumber, iron, and lime, had to be brought from considerable distances. The time it took to get them to Washington, coupled with the lack of money to pay for them, resulted in delays for which Congress turned around and blamed Latrobe.

Nevertheless, from 1803 until his resignation in 1817 it was Latrobe's vision and genius that determined the evolution of the building. He made few changes to Thornton's elevation for the East Front of the building, although the design for the handsome portico is his. The West Front was another matter. Typical of many buildings of the day (the White House, Mount Vernon, and Monticello among them), the Capitol was not designed to have a front and back. Rather, it was to have a "carriage front" on the east and a "garden front" on the west. Thornton's plan called for a semicircular colonnade and sweeping steps on the west side. Latrobe discarded that and designed instead a grand propylea, or entrance gateway, that might have been one of the masterpieces of American architecture had it been built. It was not. Latrobe's successor produced a third solution: a less flamboyant, more practical design, which included an element guaranteed to win congressional approval—space for more committee rooms.

Latrobe's major contributions were to the inside of the building. He completely redesigned Thornton's plan for the House Chamber, creating a room that was generally

acclaimed as "the most beautiful room in America." Jefferson wrote to him, telling him he was the only person in the United States capable of designing such a room, and pronouncing the room "a durable monument of your talents as an architect." The House met there for the first time on October 28, 1807. With the representatives so handsomely accommodated, Latrobe turned his attention to the Senate Chamber. He thought it undignified and inappropriate that the Senate should meet in a room on the lowest level of its wing while the representatives were meeting on a higher floor in their wing. And since the Senate wing was already in need of extensive repairs to replace rotting timbers and flaking plaster, Latrobe proposed that a major reconstruction be undertaken at the same time. He would relocate the chamber to the floor overhead, where he could also borrow from the still unfinished upper story. The lower half of the first chamber he would rebuild as a "Judiciary room," where the Supreme Court would meet. It was in this room that tragedy struck.

One of the criticisms Congress leveled at Latrobe had to do with his frequent absences from the city. He had many irons in the fire, including work on the Delaware–Chesapeake Canal, and much of the work on the Capitol was carried out by his Clerk of Works, John Lenthall, in accordance with Latrobe's written instructions. In 1808, while Latrobe was away from the city, one of the arches in what was to become the Supreme Court Chamber ceiling collapsed, killing Lenthall. It was a personal loss for Latrobe and a professional embarrassment from which he never fully recovered. Although he suggested in a confidential letter to Jefferson that Lenthall himself was partly responsible because he had removed some props prematurely, Latrobe nobly and publicly shouldered the blame himself.

By 1811 Latrobe had completed his design for the central connecting section, although next to no work had been done on it. The Senate and House wings were largely complete. Latrobe had wanted to top each wing with a cupola and had locked horns with Jefferson over this. Jefferson passionately disliked what he considered to be "an Italian invention . . . and one of the degeneracies of modern architecture," for which he could find no Greek or Roman precedent. Moreover, Jefferson claimed that Members of Congress agreed with him, which evoked the stinging retort from Latrobe: "As to the members of Congress, with the utmost respect for the Legislature, I should scarcely *consult,* but rather *dictate* in matters of taste." In vain Latrobe insisted that his cupolas were not ornamental, but utilitarian, and would admit light, but he lost that battle—at least for the time being.

Despite his considerable accomplishments, Latrobe by 1811 was increasingly frustrated in his dealings with Congress. His mentor, Jefferson, had retired and was no longer championing him. James Madison, now President, showed little interest in the building of the Capitol. The political situation between the United States and Britain was deteriorating, and money that might have gone to the various public building projects was being diverted to prepare for a war that appeared inevitable. With construction on the Capitol at a standstill, Latrobe resigned as Surveyor of Public Buildings and left Washington.

On June 18, 1812, Congress declared war on Britain. In mid-August 1814, 4,500 British army regulars landed thirty-five miles from Washington, on the Patuxent River. By August 24 they had advanced to Bladensburg, just outside the city, where they quickly overran a poorly equipped American force sent to meet them. The citizens of Washington were gathering what belongings they could and leaving the city. Among them was Dolley Madison, the President's wife, who removed Gilbert Stuart's celebrated portrait of George Washington from its frame, seized the family silver, and fled from the White House. Offices and shops closed, and the city was almost deserted by the time the British troops moved in, late on the afternoon of August 24. A letter from Latrobe to Jefferson gave an account of what happened next:

The south wing of the Capitol was set on fire with great difficulty. Of the lower story nothing could be burned but the sashes and frames, and the shutters and dressings, and the doors and door cases. As all these were detached from one another, some time and labour were necessary to get through the work. The first thing done was to empty into buckets a quantity of the composition used in the rockets. A man with an axe chopped the wood work, another followed, and brushed on some of the composition, and on retiring from each room, the third put fire to it. . . . In the House of Representatives the devastation has been dreadful. There was here no want of materials for conflagration, for when the number of members of Congress was increased, the old platform was left in its place, and another raised over it, giving an additional quantity of dry and loose timber. All the stages and seats of the galleries were of timber and yellow pine. The mahogany furniture, desks, tables and chairs, were in their places. At first they fired rockets through the roof, but they did not set fire to it. They sent men on to it, but it was covered with sheet iron. At last they made a great pile in the centre of the room of the furniture, and retiring set fire to a great quantity of rocket-stuff in the middle. The whole room was soon in a blaze. . . . In the north wing, the beautiful Doric columns which surrounded the Supreme Court room, have shared the fate of the Corinthian columns of the Hall of Representatives, and in the Senate Chamber, the marble polished columns . . . are burnt to lime, and have fallen down. . . . They stand a most magnificent ruin.

Latrobe did not mention the behavior of Rear Admiral Sir George Cockburn, commander of the British troops, who is said to have incited his men by leaping onto the Speaker's chair in the House Chamber and crying, "Shall this harbor of Yankee democracy be burned? All for it say 'aye.'" Nor did he report the heroism of his old rival, Dr. Thornton, who, according to his own account, confronted the British attackers on the stairs of the Patent Office Building. "Are you Englishmen or Goths and Vandals?" challenged Thornton. "This is the Patent Office, the depository of the inventive genius of America, in which the whole civilized world is concerned. Would you destroy it? If so, fire away and let the charge pass through my body." The Patent Office was the only government building to escape the fire, and it served as a meeting place for Congress until other quarters could be readied.

A major casualty of the fire was the total destruction of the Library of Congress, and the loss of countless documents and a few works of art. A fast-thinking Senate clerk had collected some of the Senate's records and taken them to safety at his farm in Virginia. His colleague in the House was not so swift; almost all of the

House records were lost, along with the unfortunate man's job. In a grand and generous gesture, Jefferson offered to sell to the Congress his entire private library of more than six thousand meticulously collected volumes—considerably more than had been lost in the fire. In return Congress would pay him whatever amount they saw fit, at whatever time they wished. He stipulated only that the collection be kept intact, and that he be allowed to keep a few mathematical and scientific books "to amuse the time [he had] yet to pass." Congress accepted his offer, and got a good bargain for the $23,950 it paid. Some of those books were lost in a subsequent fire, but a part of the collection has survived and is today in the Rare Book and Special Collections Division of the Library of Congress.

Only a heavy summer rain prevented the Capitol from being more severely damaged that night. As it was, the damage was so extensive that Latrobe, who was recalled to Washington the following year to undertake the re-

pairs of the building, wrote to Jefferson: "At a less expense to the U States, a much more convenient, & magnificent building could have been erected, than will be made of the ruins of the former." Had that happened, however, the pressure to move the capital to another city would certainly have been intense; now, in addition to its slow development and many inconveniences, events had proved that Washington was a poorly defended city. The citizens therefore lost no time in organizing a movement to ensure that the government stayed. Bankers offered a $500,000 loan for reconstructing the damaged buildings, and a group of leading Washingtonians raised a subscription to build the "Brick Capitol" as a temporary meeting place for Congress while repairs to the Capitol were being made. That the new building was up and running within six months attests to their determination not to let the government leave. The three-story building stood on the site now occupied by the Supreme Court; it housed the Senate, House of Representatives, Supreme Court, and Circuit Court of the District of Columbia until the Capitol could be reoccupied. It later served as a prison for Southern sympathizers during the Civil War, and was razed in 1867.

The fire had underscored the need for fireproof construction, and much of Latrobe's work after the fire was directed toward that end. Brick and stone replaced wood to the extent possible. It helped that President Monroe was eager to complete the building, and Congress was generous with appropriations. The Senate Chamber was enlarged, and the House Chamber was redesigned as a semicircular room with a half-dome; these two rooms exist today as the Old Senate Chamber and Statuary Hall, respectively. And with Jefferson's attention now focused on other pursuits at Monticello, the wings were rebuilt with domes and cupolas.

In 1816 the three commissioners for the District of Columbia had been replaced by a sole commissioner, Samuel Lane. This official accused Latrobe of spending too much money, and the increasingly public friction between them forced Latrobe to tender his resignation the following year. In resigning, Latrobe complained to Jefferson that Lane treated him worse than he (Latrobe) treated his mechanics. He justified all his expenditures at the Capitol, and denied that he had been wasteful. He expressed his respect for President Monroe, but said he was "well aware of the course of intrigue that suddenly induced him to forbid me all approach to him personally and by letter. He will be undeceived, tho' perhaps too late. . . ." Once again, the creative man had crossed swords with the well-connected.

Even before Latrobe's resignation had been tendered, President Monroe had met and decided upon his successor. Charles Bulfinch was to be the first American-born architect to work on the Capitol. Educated at Harvard, he had become interested in architecture while in Europe and had practiced it as an avocation on his return to the United States. A failed business had forced him to turn to it professionally, and he had built a thriving practice in his native Boston, designing churches, hospitals, and public buildings for various states and counties. He was considered to have "good judgment and refinement,"

and to be a sensible and selfless member of society. His integrity was nowhere better shown than in his refusal to seek the plum that he knew could be his until the incumbent had chosen to resign: "I have always endeavored to avoid unpleasant competition with others. . . . I should much regret being the instrument of depriving a man of undoubted talents of employment which places him at the head of his profession." Latrobe handed in his resignation on November 20, 1817, and Bulfinch arrived in Washington in January 1818.

What made Bulfinch the right man for the job was that he was not too proud to devote himself wholeheartedly to the scrupulous completion of another's plan, even when he disagreed with aspects of it. At the same time, however, he possessed the talent to create appropriate and harmonious designs for those areas in which he was given a freer rein. The pressing need in 1818 was to get the two chambers ready for occupancy. The Senate and the House were able to return to the Capitol in December 1819, and by the following year the Senate and House wings were essentially finished.

Where Bulfinch could make his greatest contribution was in the central part of the building. It was still little more than some old and abandoned foundations when the first appropriation for its construction ($100,000) was made in 1818, and on August 24 of that year, four years to the day after the British had burned the building, the cornerstone for the final section was laid. Both Thornton and Latrobe had made drawings for the central part, but Bulfinch changed them quite substantially. He also radically altered the dome Thornton had designed. It was a relatively low one, and criticism against it had been widespread, coming even from such influential people as President Monroe and Secretary of State John Quincy Adams, who thought that the most important building in the nation deserved a correspondingly lofty dome. Bulfinch submitted a series of proposals featuring domes of increasing and even (in his opinion) inappropriate height. His own preference was for moderation, and he was taken aback and not altogether pleased when the President not only selected the highest one he had drawn, but intimated that it might have been higher still. Bulfinch never liked the dome, and did what he could to have it made lower, even as it was being built. But the lesson of his predecessors' quarrels had not been wasted on

him. The wooden dome, sheathed with copper, rose as high as the President wanted it to.

Bulfinch also altered Latrobe's more grandiose plan for the West Front, creating the restrained and dignified exterior that exists today. Finally, in 1826 he completed the East Portico, according to Latrobe's plans. He spent the next three years working on details both inside and outside the building, including sculpture, landscaping, and gatehouses for the Capitol grounds. On March 4, 1829, Andrew Jackson became the first President to be inaugurated on the East Front. Two months later the office of Architect of the Capitol was abolished, and the following year Bulfinch returned to Boston. Thirty-six years after the laying of the cornerstone, the building of the United States Capitol, based on Thornton's design, had been completed.

The building of the nation which the Capitol served, however, was anything but complete. The next two decades, 1830 to 1850, were to be years of enormous expansion. A treaty with Britain in 1846 secured the Oregon Territory, which included Oregon, Washington, Idaho, and parts of Montana. Texas had entered the Union in 1845, bringing with it an ongoing border dispute with Mexico that precipitated the outbreak of the Mexican War in 1846. As a result of the war, land from Texas to California was added to the United States' territories, which now stretched from the Gulf of Mexico to the Pacific. By 1850 immigrants were flooding into the country and many were making their way westward. Between the time when Thornton had drawn his original plan

and the year 1850, the number of states in the Union had more than doubled. Instead of thirty senators there were now sixty-two, and the House had grown from sixty-nine members to 233. For most congressmen, their desks still served as their entire allotment of office space; constituents who wanted to get their representative's ear often did so in the Senate or House Chamber, and the scene was at times chaotic. It was obvious that the building was too small. When Jefferson Davis introduced an amendment to an appropriations bill in 1850, authorizing the construction of an addition and $100,000 with which to build it, the measure passed with little debate.

In 1836 Andrew Jackson appointed Robert Mills as architect and superintendent of construction of the new Treasury Building. Mills, however, preferred the title "Architect of Public Buildings." He was a protégé of Jefferson's, and had studied engineering and architecture with Latrobe. He was more than competent (he was the original architect of the Washington Monument), and as Architect of Public Buildings he took it upon himself to draw up plans for the expansion of the Capitol. The Senate, however, was determined to follow the precedent of 1792, and another competition was duly announced in 1850. It called for a plan to enlarge the building either by adding wings to the north and south, or by erecting a separate building to the east. The prize was again to be $500, but this time, drawing on past experience, it was wisely stipulated that entries could be adapted and combined, with the prize money being split accordingly. There was no clear winner, and the eventual solution, which called for two new wings, borrowed features from a number of designs, including Mills's. The prize was divided five ways, and President Millard Fillmore appointed one of the contestants, Thomas U. Walter, Architect of the Capitol Extension.

Walter was a prominent Philadelphia architect, and ideally suited for the job. Like Bulfinch, he was a man of discrimination and good taste who understood and appreciated classical design. He had little inclination toward self-promotion, and could be relied upon to treat the old building with the sensitivity it merited. On July 4, 1851, in front of some who had attended the first cornerstone ceremony in 1793, a third cornerstone was laid in the Capitol. The symbolism was noted: the old building stood for the old Union, firm and unbroken, while the new wings represented the new states—such as Texas and California—coming in and uniting themselves with the old. Then, in an address lasting two hours, Daniel Webster made an emotional plea for national unity:

> If, therefore, it shall be hereafter the will of God that this structure shall fall from its base, that its foundation be upturned, and his deposit brought to the eyes of men, be it then known, that on this day the Union of the United States of America stands firm, that their Constitution still exists unimpaired, and with all its original usefulness and glory; growing every day stronger and stronger in the affections of the great body of the American people, and attracting more and more the admiration of the world. And all here assembled, whether belonging to public life or to private life, with hearts devoutly thankful to Almighty God for the preservation of the liberty and happiness of the country, unite in sincere and fervent prayers that this deposit, and the walls and arches, the domes and towers, the columns and entablatures, now to be erected over it, may endure for ever!

Walter deposited a copy of Webster's speech, newspapers of the day, coins, and other mementos in a sealed jar within the cornerstone, and construction was under way.

Walter's plans called for adding wings at right angles to the existing building and connected to it by narrow corridors. Marble from Massachusetts and Maryland was to be used in place of sandstone for the new wings, thus at least partially realizing Thornton's original aspirations for the building. The new wings would house the badly needed larger chambers for both the Senate and the House. This, however, left the question of what to do with the old chambers. It was decided to make the old Senate Chamber into the Supreme Court Chamber; the old Supreme Court Chamber would in turn become the Law Library. Those chambers exist today as two of the three "museum" rooms in the Capitol. The old House Chamber posed a more difficult dilemma. Few had the heart to subdivide such a handsome room, and yet it was too large for any practical purpose. Various proposals were put forward, but for lack of any one of them being adopted the room soon degenerated into little better than a dusty storage area. In 1864 Representative Justin

On display in the crypt is a Corinthian capital from the east front's original sandstone columns. The plaster model for the capitals was carved under the direction of Giovanni Andrei, one of the sculptors brought over from Carrara, Italy, in 1806 by Latrobe at the urging of Thomas Jefferson. Carved on site, each capital took one man six months' work.

Morrill of Vermont introduced a bill ordering that the room be "set apart for the reception of such statuary as each State shall elect to be deserving of this lasting commemoration." The old Hall of the House was thus reborn as National Statuary Hall, the third museum room in the Capitol. All three old chambers were painstakingly restored in time for the celebration of the Bicentennial in 1976.

On Christmas Eve, 1851, a few months after the cornerstone ceremony, a spark from a stove started a fire in the Library of Congress. A fire engine was rushed into the Rotunda, and President Fillmore is said to have seen the flames from the White House and hurried along to the Capitol to lend a hand. The damage was substantial: 35,000 books and manuscripts—the major part of the Library's collection—

SECTION through DOME of U.S. CAPITOL

Thomas u. walter's revised 1859 drawing shows the "double" dome and the immense painting he planned for the canopy, inspired by the panthéon in paris. (architect of the capitol)

ningly exhibited in his office a drawing showing the Capitol with a much larger and more elaborate dome. Such was the reaction of all who saw it that in less than three months, with unprecedented rapidity, the House, the Senate, and President Franklin Pierce had not only accepted Walter's idea, but had also appropriated $100,000, which they thought were the necessary funds. It was about one tenth of what the final cost would be.

Walter designed a cast-iron "double" dome, with an inner and outer shell, inspired by St. Paul's Cathedral in London, the Panthéon in Paris, and St. Isaac's Cathedral in St. Petersburg. It was to be widely copied afterward in state capitals across the United States. Nearly twice the height of the original dome, its construction is still today considered a feat of engineering. More than five

were lost, along with sculptures and priceless portraits of the first five Presidents by Gilbert Stuart. The fire did underscore the imperative of using fireproof materials, however, as indeed subsequent events have shown. A gas explosion outside the Supreme Court Chamber in 1898 might well have destroyed the entire building but for the fireproof building materials. In reconstructing the Library, Walter produced the first room in America built of cast iron (thought at that time to be a fireproof material). Even the bookshelves were made of iron. Iron was also used for the ceilings of the chambers, for all window and door trims in the extension, and for the towering new dome that was to become Walter's most celebrated contribution to the Capitol.

The new wings under construction more than doubled the length of the building. At the same time they gave Bulfinch's dome, in the words of Representative Richard Stanton, "a squatty appearance." Moreover, it leaked and was a fire hazard. Walter knew it had to go, and cun-

million pounds of masonry were laid on top of the Rotunda walls to support the columns of the peristyle, and nearly nine million pounds of cast iron were used in the dome's construction. An intricate grid of trusses, girders, and bolts counteracts the expansion and contraction—as much as four inches—caused by changes in temperature.

Atop the dome stands a nineteen-and-a-half-foot bronze statue, variously referred to as "Armed Liberty" and "Freedom Triumphant in War and Peace," but affectionately known simply as "Freedom." "Freedom" holds in her right hand a sheathed sword, indicating both a state of peace and, at the same time, a readiness to defend that peace if called upon. In her left hand she holds a laurel wreath of victory and the shield of the United States. She stands on an iron globe, around which is cast the national motto, *E Pluribus Unum.* Designed in Rome by Thomas Crawford, who died before his model could be shipped, "Freedom" narrowly survived a calamitous voyage from Italy to New York, and finally reached

Washington in 1859. The statue was cast in bronze at a foundry near Washington, and when the outer dome was almost completed the five sections of the statue were lifted, one by one, into position. On December 2, 1863, the last section—the head and shoulders—was put in place. Despite the ongoing Civil War, a fitting ceremony was planned for the occasion; a 35-gun salute was fired from a battery on the Capitol grounds—one gun for each state then in the Union, including the Confederate states. Walter's instructions to the superintendent for the day's events stipulated that there be no noise, waving of hats, or attempt by anyone at speech-making, and concluded with the sensible injunction: "You are further directed to permit no one to get up on the head after it is up."

The magnificent new dome had only one noticeable defect. Walter had set out to design the largest dome possible for the building, and in order to do this the columns of the peristyle surrounding the drum of the dome had to be cantilevered out on brackets. On the East Front the columns appeared to loom over the void of the portico, giving the impression from some angles that the dome was inadequately supported. Walter himself was aware of the problem and proposed extending the East Front to correct it, but it would be almost a century before resistance to tampering with what was already being viewed as a national treasure could be overcome and the work begun.

True to past tradition, Walter too was to have his nemesis, who soon appeared in the person of Montgomery Cunningham Meigs, an engineer, self-taught architect, and

military officer. In 1853 the responsibility for the construction of the Capitol had been transferred from the Interior Department to the War Department, and Jefferson Davis, then Secretary of War, appointed Meigs to be Superintendent of Construction of the Capitol. As such he was responsible for various engineering aspects, such as heating, ventilation, and acoustics, but he also had authority to award contracts and disburse funds, and this he did with an imperious autonomy that soon antagonized Congress. At first Walter and Meigs worked well together, but their artistic views were at such variance—and Meigs's manner was so peremptory—that a falling-out was inevitable. The two men began to complain about each other to the Secretary of War, and even to the President himself. In Jefferson Davis, Meigs had a powerful champion, but when Davis was replaced, Meigs's position became tenuous. He then demanded that Walter turn over to him all the drawings, a demand that Walter not only refused but countered with an offer of immediate and willing resignation. Walter was allowed to keep both the drawings and his position, but after one complaint too many, Meigs was relieved of his duty on November 1, 1859.

His domineering manner notwithstanding, Meigs was conscientious and able. During his tenure, work on the two wings progressed with a minimum of delays; the House was able to hold its first legislative session in its new chamber on December 16, 1857, and the Senate moved into its new home on January 4, 1859. Furthermore, most of the changes Meigs proposed were improvements. It was his idea to

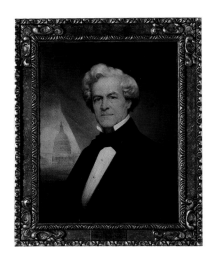

have each chamber in the center of its respective wing, rather than at the western end, as previously planned. This change allowed committee rooms and other offices for the many varied functions of the legislature to be located conveniently around the chambers. In general Meigs tended to favor an elaborate style; it was one of the points on which he and Walter disagreed. It was to be expected that in awarding commissions for the art in the Capitol he would make as many enemies as friends. In particular, a marked animus against foreigners began to develop because most of the artists and craftsmen working on the Capitol were foreign-born. In 1859 a petition was circulated, with Rembrandt Peale's the first signature on it, demanding that only American artists be permitted to work in the Capitol. Meigs, however, was

uncompromising; to him competence was more important than national origin. In deciding who should receive commissions he did meticulous research both as to the artists and sculptors, and as to the media they should use. He was intrigued with the idea of using fresco to decorate the walls, a technique not yet much used in the United States. When, then, an Italian painter asked to be allowed to try his hand at this, Meigs invited him to produce a sample of his work in his own office—a room that was shortly to be turned over to the House Committee on Agriculture.

Meigs's gamble paid off. Of all the artists whom he brought into the Capitol, none labored longer, nor with more heart, than Constantino Brumidi. A political refugee from Italy, from the day in 1855 on which he first began to work in the Capitol until his death twenty-five years later, he had but one ambition: "to live long enough to make beautiful the Capitol of the one country on earth in which there is liberty." He was to die while pursuing his goal. Working tirelessly and continually, Brumidi decorated walls and ceilings in rooms and corridors. He painted portraits and commemorated events and achievements in oil and fresco. He completed what is undoubtedly his chef d'oeuvre, *The Apotheosis of Washington,* the immense fresco over the eye of the dome. He designed and was working on the frescoed frieze almost sixty feet above the floor of the Rotunda and had completed about a third of it when disaster struck. He fell backward, and although he was able to cling to the scaffolding until help came, the shock was too great for the seventy-four-year-old man; he died four and a half months later.

Ironically, even as the Capitol was being enlarged to accommodate a larger Congress, events on the political front were moving toward making the additional space sadly unnecessary. Relations between the North and the South over the issue of slavery had deteriorated greatly during the 1850s. In 1856 Massachusetts Senator Charles

Top: THOMAS U. WALTER, BY FRANCISCO PAUSAS AFTER A MATHEW BRADY PHOTOGRAPH. WALTER WAS APPOINTED ARCHITECT OF THE CAPITOL EXTENSION IN 1851 AND UNDER HIS DIRECTION THE BUILDING MORE THAN DOUBLED IN SIZE. *BOTTOM:* A GROUP OF SPECTATORS WATCH THE HOISTING OF A COLUMN SHAFT INTO PLACE, HOUSE CONNECTING CORRIDOR, NOVEMBER 1860. (*ARCHITECT OF THE CAPITOL*)

Sumner, a passionate opponent of slavery, had been savagely attacked at his desk in the Senate Chamber by Representative Preston Brooks, a relative of South Carolina's aging Senator Andrew Butler, whom Sumner had denounced in a speech. It was not uncommon for Members to arm themselves against threats of assassination by carrying weapons even into the Capitol. By 1860, the high hopes and expectations the senators had carried with them into their new chamber the year before were in disarray, and in December South Carolina became the first state to secede from the Union. Early in 1861 Jefferson Davis, accompanied by four Southern colleagues, brought tears to the eyes of those in the packed chamber and galleries with an eloquent and moving farewell speech, before proceeding somberly out of the chamber for the last time. Within a few weeks eleven states had approved ordinances of secession; the Senate had been reduced from sixty-six members to fifty, the House of Representatives from 237 to 178. And the Civil War had begun.

With the war came a period in the history of the Capitol that could never have been foreseen by those architects and statesmen who had labored to create it. In the spring of 1861 the Capitol was taken over for use as a temporary barracks for as many as 3,000 Northern troops, who referred to it as the "Big Tent." An emergency hospital was set up, ovens were built in the basement, and flour was stored in the Crypt. Bacon was hung in some of the country's most handsome rooms. Congress quickly protested the Capitol being used in such a way, while the Librarian of Congress worried that smoke from the ovens was damaging his books. Poor Walter found it impossible to work, writing ruefully in a letter:

> The drummers' drill is right under my windows; — there are about 100 drummers all the time drumming, having a head drummer to teach them; they have been going over the same *toodle-dee, toodle-dee, toodle-dee, too* for the last two hours, and that on at least 100 drums—this is a great place.

In the fall of that year President Lincoln ordered the occupation to cease and the building to be repaired and readied for the next session of Congress. The turmoil of

CONSTRUCTION OF THE DOME CONTINUED DURING THE CIVIL WAR; UNION SOLDIERS ARE VISIBLE IN THE FOREGROUND OF THIS 1861 PHOTOGRAPH. (*ARCHITECT OF THE CAPITOL*)

the war had caused construction on the building to come to a halt in May 1861; Congress ordered it resumed a year later. Only work on the dome continued uninterrupted; the contractors doing the work had 1.3 million pounds of iron, at seven cents a pound, lying in readiness next to the Capitol, as well as a completion clause in their contract. In 1863 Lincoln made the memorable comment: "If the people see this Capitol going on, they will know that we intend the Union shall go on." Only two years later, Abraham Lincoln would lie in state in the Rotunda under the nearly completed dome.

Shortly after Lincoln's death, Walter resigned, piqued by what he considered an abrogation of his authority by the Secretary of the Interior, who had summarily dismissed a contractor hired by Walter. It was yet another case of conflict between the artistic and the political temperament. Walter left with dignity and returned to Philadelphia to practice architecture. He was replaced by Edward Clark, who held the job of Architect of the Capitol until 1902. Clark was a man of broad artistic, scientific, and literary interests, and a generous patron of many institutions. Under his direction the expansion begun by Walter was completed, and by 1868 the exterior of the Capitol appeared much as it does today.

What remained to be done was the continuing work of modernizing the interior of the building. In 1874 the first elevator was installed in the Senate wing (by then two disabled Civil War veterans had been elected to Congress). An experiment in 1880 to replace the gas lighting with electricity was not an unqualified success because the light was found to be too unsteady for the chambers, but by the turn of the century the building had been completely electrified. In 1893 modern plumbing replaced the earlier primitive system.

On the outside, stables and other temporary buildings were removed. In 1873 the grounds surrounding the Capitol were enlarged by closing both A streets—on the north and south. In 1874 Frederick Law Olmsted, the foremost landscape architect of the period and the designer of New York's Central Park, was put in charge of landscaping the Capitol Grounds.

History, however, was to repeat itself. Twenty years after Thornton's original Capitol had been built it was already too small; twenty years after Walter's new wings had been added the building had again been outgrown. There were thirty states in the Union when the expansion was planned; by 1890 there were forty-four. Moreover, during the 1880s Congress had enacted legislation authorizing each Member to maintain a personal staff of one. Although niggardly by today's standards, it guaranteed a continuing need for still more space. For the most part that need would be met by the construction of congressional office buildings. The first House Office Building opened in 1908; there are now three House and three Senate office buildings, along with a number of annexes. Taken all together, they have vastly increased the working area of the Congress.

It was the still unresolved matter of the dome that would bring the aesthetes and the pragmatists together. Its position over the eastern portico continued to rankle architects and laymen alike. In 1958, with powerful congressional support, authorization to extend the central area of the East Front and the connecting corridors by 32 feet was secured. In addition to restoring the architectural integrity of the building, the extension would result in the creation of more than ninety new rooms. Using the same trowel and gavel that George Washington and Millard Fillmore had used, President Eisenhower laid a fourth cornerstone on July 4, 1959. Under the supervision of George Stewart, then Architect of the Capitol, the existing sandstone facade became an interior wall, but it was faithfully and meticulously replicated in more durable domestic marble for the new East Front. Bulfinch's sandstone columns were also replaced with marble. Twenty-two of the twenty-four original columns now stand in the National Arboretum, but one of the original Corinthian capitals—which took one man six months to carve in 1825—is permanently on display in the Crypt. This last major enlargement of the Capitol was sufficiently completed in time for President Kennedy to be inaugurated on the finished East Front in 1961.

In 1971 George M. White was appointed Architect of the Capitol, the ninth man to occupy the position. Architect, engineer, and lawyer, White has been responsible for implementing many of the technological advances called for by the Congress during the last twenty years, including electronic voting in the House Chamber, surveillance systems, television coverage of House and Senate debates, and computer and communication facilities. Perhaps his greatest challenge, however, was the rapidly deteriorating condition of the sandstone wall of the central West Front. This had been of concern since the 1960s, and only disagreement over the best way to restore it had delayed any work being done on it. The collapse of a section of the sandstone veneer in 1983 lent new urgency to the problem, and in what was the most difficult restoration project on the building to date, White replaced about a third of the original Aquia Creek sandstone with Indiana limestone, reinforced the foundation, and installed insulated glass in the windows—taking care to preserve every detail of the existing appearance of the building. The central section of the West Front is the only facade of the building where some of the original Aquia Creek sandstone is still to be seen.

Quite possibly the Capitol will never be "finished," and perhaps that is as it should be. Architectural historian Glenn Brown wrote at the beginning of the twentieth century: "Repairs to and alterations of the Capitol have been continuously made, and will be so long as the nation lives and grows. When such alterations cease, the nation will be on the decline." Certainly a building of such monumental scale must be in a constant state of renovation and alteration. During the final decade of the twentieth century White began the work of restoring

WHEN THE EAST FRONT OF THE CAPITOL WAS EXTENDED, BULFINCH'S SANDSTONE COLUMNS WERE REPLACED WITH MARBLE. TWENTY-TWO OF THE TWENTY-FOUR ORIGINAL COLUMNS HAVE BEEN ERECTED IN THE NATIONAL ARBORETUM, ARRANGED IN A CONFIGURATION THAT EVOKES THEIR FORMER LOCATION AND PRESENTS A HAUNTING REMINDER OF THE EARLY LIFE OF THE CAPITOL.

the Olmsted terraces, which had deteriorated, and converting the courtyards into, not surprisingly, more meeting space. It is safe to predict, however, that there will be no significant changes to the outward appearance of the Capitol in the future. It has evolved into a magnificent building, satisfying to both the eye and the hearts of its owners, the American people.

Thornton could no more have dreamed what his Capitol would eventually look like than Washington could have conceived what kind of a nation his would become. Within the walls of the Capitol is carried on the daunting business of governing a nation of people as diverse as ever existed. In its legislative chambers every shade of opinion can be heard, every contradictory belief expressed. Yet above those legislative chambers towers that magnificent symbol of unity, the dome. And crowning that, Freedom keeps watch, "presiding over the whole and viewing the first rays of the rising, and the last rays of the setting sun." [Meigs] Over the course of its two-hundred-year history the United States Capitol has grown, sometimes fitfully and sometimes gracefully, from being the mere symbol of an idea—the idea of government by the people—to being a cherished monument that embodies the nation's rich remembrance of the past and high hopes for the future. In that respect, it is timeless.

A MONUMENT
HIGH AND
ALONE

IN SELECTING Jenkins Hill as the location for the Capitol, Pierre L'Enfant had made an excellent choice. Capitol Hill, as it is now known, rises 88 feet above the level of the Potomac, and the Capitol, with the statue of "Freedom" sitting atop it, towers another 287 feet 5½ inches above that. It is a landmark almost impossible to miss. Visitors arriving in Washington by train emerge from Union Station with the massive dome directly ahead of them. Flights into National Airport touch down only three miles from the Capitol, and they often afford spectacular views of the building on their final approach. Motorists from points north, south, and east have the Capitol in sight well before they reach the heart of the city. Only from the west is the building more elusive, except for a tantalizing glimpse from high above the Potomac just west of the Francis Scott Key Bridge: the river sweeps down to the Watergate, beyond which the Washington Monument rises, and far off in the distance the familiar dome comes into view. ∼ It is a sight that has moved even well-traveled skeptics. Frances Trollope, the mother of the English novelist, wrote in 1833: ∼ "Our first object the next morning was to get a sight of the capitol, and our impatience sent us forth before breakfast. The mists of morning still hung

CROWNING THE CAPITOL
DOME, THE BRONZE STATUE OF
FREEDOM VIEWS "THE FIRST
RAYS OF THE RISING, AND THE
LAST RAYS OF THE SETTING
SUN." *FACING PAGE:* MOONRISE
BEHIND THE DOME.

The capitol dome from union station. For decades after the first train arrived there in 1907 and until the advent of air travel, Union Station was the principal gateway to Washington; many a visitor caught a first glimpse of the Capitol Dome through its arches. Noted architect Daniel H. Burnham, a member of the McMillan Commission of 1902 and a man whose credo was "make no little plans," designed the superb neoclassical station. The interior was inspired by the Baths of Diocletian in Rome.

around this magnificent building when first it broke upon our view, and I am not sure that the effect produced was not the greater for this circumstance. At all events, we were struck with admiration and surprise. None of us, I believe, expected to see so imposing a structure on that side [of] the Atlantic. I am ill at describing buildings, but the beauty and majesty of the American capitol might defy an abler pen than mine to do it justice. It stands so finely too, high, and alone. . . . The view from the capitol commands the city and many miles around, and it is itself an object of imposing beauty to the whole country adjoining. (*The Domestic Manners of the Americans*)

The Capitol still stands high and alone. Of all American cities, only Washington has resisted the temptation to build upward, the city fathers having determined in the late nineteenth century that they preferred streets lit by sunlight to the canyon-like thoroughfares being built in cities like New York and Chicago. For years an unwritten convention governed the height of Washington buildings, but in 1910 Congress passed an Act effectively restricting buildings throughout the city to a height of 130 feet, or 160 feet along Pennsylvania Avenue, which was deemed wide enough to accommodate taller buildings. The main purpose of the Act was to protect for all time the visual prominence of both the Capitol and the Washington Monument.

In situating the Capitol at the intersection of twelve radiating avenues,

Pierre L'Enfant expected to be creating at least a dozen good angles from which to observe it, and to a large extent he succeeded. The view from one of them, however, would have sorely disappointed him. Pennsylvania Avenue was planned to be the principal thoroughfare of the city, and was so named as a gesture of respect to the last state to house the Congress before it moved to its permanent home. The avenue was envisioned as a grand and ceremonial link between the Capitol and the White House—an American Champs-Elysées. But in 1833 the old Treasury Building near the White House burned down, and three years of congressional wrangling over where to rebuild it ensued. Exasperated, President Andrew Jackson is said to have finally taken matters into his

own hands, walked out of the White House, planted his cane in the ground, and ordered the Treasury to be built "right here." The story that he added something about wanting the building to block his view of an uncooperative Congress may well be apocryphal; in any case, it was not immediately apparent that the building would do so. Only after the Treasury was going up did Congress fully realize just how large it would be, and by the time anything could be done about getting it redesigned or relocated, the expense of doing either had become prohibitive. Today a small part of the southern end of the Treasury effectively obliterates L'Enfant's plan for an uninterrupted vista between the Capitol and White House. No doubt L'Enfant would have known what to do about that, but he was long gone.

Of the twelve approaches, by far the most magnificent views of the Capitol are to be had from any point along the broad Mall, which extends from the foot of Capitol Hill west toward the Washington Monument, the Lincoln Memorial, and Arlington Cemetery. The disposition of buildings and monuments along the length of the Mall is all that an artist could ask for, but even mightier forces are at work. Since the Mall runs east to west, early-morning strollers see the sun rise behind the Capitol, often with dramatic effects in the sky and on the building. Moonrise can be equally breathtaking. When the sun sets, at the opposite end of the Mall, its refracted rays bathe the white marble of the building in a swiftly changing palette ranging from gold to crimson.

The Mall today is not as L'Enfant envisioned it. He planned grand houses and embassies on either side, with spacious gardens—an area that would be lively with people day and night. That was never realized, and by the end of the nineteenth century the Mall was quite simply a mess. In 1873 the Pennsylvania Railroad had been allowed to build a station directly on it, with accompanying sheds, tracks, and coal yards. A polluted canal ran across the Mall, and sections of it were prone to flooding. In 1900 a Senate Park Commission was formed, headed by Senator James McMillan of Michigan, and it recommended and carried out a return to L'Enfant's basic ideas. Today the canal has been filled in, Tiber Creek runs underground, and the Mall is an enormous expanse of green, flanked not by houses but by museums and art galleries. It is punctuated by the Lincoln Memorial and the Washington Monument and by reflecting pools and gardens. It is the public heart of the city.

The visitor approaching the Capitol from the Mall unknowingly crosses a major interstate highway that runs underground along the base of Capitol Hill. Concealing the path of I-395 is a large reflecting pool, whose placid surface faithfully reproduces the image of the giant building beyond it.

The Capitol Grounds—nearly sixty acres of carefully tended gardens—begin on the east side of the reflecting pool. More than one

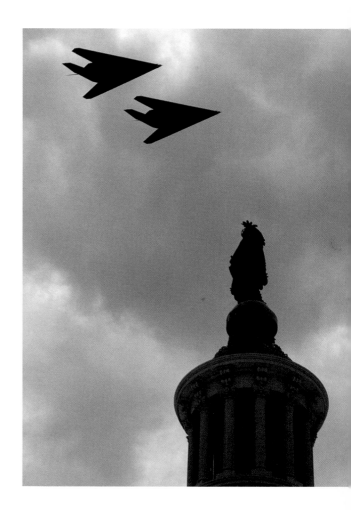

$\mathcal{A}$ CONCERT GIVEN BY WASH-
INGTON'S NATIONAL SYMPHONY
ORCHESTRA ON THE WEST LAWN
OF THE CAPITOL IN CONJUNC-
TION WITH THE DESERT STORM
VICTORY CELEBRATIONS. *PAGES
56-57:* THE CELEBRATIONS
LASTED FROM JUNE 6 TO JUNE
10, 1991, BRINGING AN ESTI-
MATED 800,000 PEOPLE TO
WATCH THE NATIONAL VICTORY
PARADE AND FIREWORKS. AN
UNPRECEDENTED DISPLAY OF
MILITARY HARDWARE WAS AS-
SEMBLED ON THE MALL, BEGIN-
NING WITH THE DAWN ARRIVAL
OF THE VERTICAL TAKE-OFF
AND LANDING HARRIER JET
(AV-8B) AND ACCOMPANYING
HELICOPTERS, *LEFT.* EIGHTY-
THREE WARPLANES STAGED A
FLYOVER ABOVE THE CAPITOL
DOME, CLIMAXED BY THE AP-
PEARANCE OF TWO OMINOUS-
LOOKING STEALTH BOMBERS
(F-117A), WHOSE DEAFENING
ROAR REVERBERATED LONG
AFTER THEY HAD DISAPPEARED,
TOP RIGHT. THE CELEBRATIONS
OVER, THE HARRIER WAS THE
LAST TO LEAVE; IT LIFTED
SLOWLY OFF THE GROUND,
HOVERED, THEN QUICKLY
GAINED SPEED TO SOAR DOWN
THE MALL, *BOTTOM RIGHT.*

hundred varieties of trees and shrubs grow here, many bearing historic associations and some representing various states, including a giant sequoia from California. The layout of the grounds was the work of the preeminent American landscape architect Frederick Law Olmsted. The addition of the Capitol's two wings in the 1850s created a need to enlarge the grounds immediately surrounding the building to provide an appropriate setting, and in 1874 Olmsted was commissioned to undertake the task. Prior to that the land around the Capitol had received only scant attention. During the years when the Capitol was being built the grounds were littered with sheds, stables, shops and barracks for the workers, and stockpiles of building materials. Animals roamed over it freely, and any attempts to landscape it were inexpert and short-lived. Olmsted charitably described the

state of the grounds as he found them as one of "sylvan juvenility" and proceeded to produce a plan that included broad lawns, curving walkways, vibrant seasonal plantings, and a grotto fed with springwater. His intention was to balance the cold white marble of the building with as much verdure as he could. In the 1820s Bulfinch had put a fence around the grounds to keep stray animals out; with that problem solved, Olmsted was able to replace the fence with a low wall without gates—a more aesthetic and fitting enclosure for a building that was intended to be open to the people to whom it belonged. In addition to his landscaping work, Olmsted turned his attention to the West Front. There the addition of the new wings had reduced the existing earthen terraces to insignificance in relation to the size of the building they supported. Olmsted designed the marble terrace that now bears his name and the grand staircases on the West Front.

In the center of the Capitol Rotunda the north-south and east-west axes of the city intersect; from this point the four quadrants of the city—northwest, northeast, southeast, and southwest—are marked out. While the Capitol is not the geographic center of the city, it is certainly the symbolic center. More than any other building, it defines Washington's raison d'être. In a city offering literally dozens of tourist attractions, the Capitol is the foremost destination of millions of visitors annually. It is at once a museum, an art gallery, and a working office building.

THE MOON BEHIND THE STATUE OF FREEDOM SHOWS THE LATENESS OF THE HOUR, BUT THE LIGHT IN THE LANTERN OF THE THOLOS SIGNIFIES THAT CONGRESS IS STILL IN SESSION—A TRADITION BEGUN WHEN THE FIRST GASLIGHT WAS LIT IN THE NEWLY COMPLETED DOME. FACING PAGE: THE NATION'S BICENTENNIAL CELEBRATIONS DREW HUNDREDS OF THOUSANDS OF VISITORS TO THE CAPITAL. CROWDS AROUND THE REFLECTING POOL AT THE LINCOLN MEMORIAL WERE SO DENSE THAT SOME SOUGHT BREATHING SPACE BY WADING INTO THE POOL, FULLY CLOTHED.

Left: DETAILS OF THE DOME
AND COLUMNS AND PEDIMENT
OF THE HOUSE WING, EAST
FRONT. *RIGHT:* THE MARBLE
PEACE MONUMENT, ERECTED
AT THE FOOT OF CAPITOL HILL
IN MEMORY OF THE NAVY MEN
WHO DIED DURING THE CIVIL
WAR, SHOWS AMERICA WEEP-
ING ON THE SHOULDER OF
HISTORY. IT WAS SCULPTED IN
ROME BY FRANKLIN SIMMONS.

As the supreme symbol of American democracy, the Capitol serves as the focal point for both celebrations and protests. Each Fourth of July the Capitol serves as the backdrop for ever more dramatic pyrotechnical displays. In June 1991 the Desert Storm victory was celebrated with a great parade, at the climax of which scores of aircraft, representing every kind that had taken part in the Gulf War, thundered in formation over the Capitol dome, streaking down the Mall and out of sight across the Potomac River. Citizens with grievances to air will often choose to do so on the highly visible steps of the Capitol. There protesters against the war in Vietnam were a familiar sight and the flag burners got the attention they sought. What is remarkable is that protesters do not seem out of place there. They are, after all, one of the reasons the building exists. Lyndon Johnson said, "Our house is large, and it is open. It is open to all, those who agree and those who dissent." The Capitol belongs to the American people, and in it and around it their voices may be heard.

ENTRANCES
AND
PORTICOES

THE appearance the Capitol has today, its symmetry and integrity, belies the fact that it has evolved and grown over nearly two hundred years, under the charge of nine Architects of the Capitol and the sometimes fortuitous, sometimes inept, involvement of Presidents, superintendents, commissioners, engineers, and politicians. Nor has this integrity been achieved at the expense of the old-fashioned or the outgrown. Even in an earlier age, when historic restoration was perhaps less valued than it is today, certain elements of the building were lovingly retained, restored, and even recycled. The first part of the building to be completed and occupied, the old north wing, is still there, and although it is now dwarfed by Walter's extension and the dome, it takes only a little imagination to see how the Capitol appeared to George Washington. ❧ The wings added by Thomas U. Walter in the 1850s have Corinthian columns and pilasters that are similar to those on the original building. There are three porticoes on the east side, and the sculptural groups in the three pediments are harmonious, despite the fact that they were executed by three different sculptors over a period of nearly a century. ❧ Of the three, the central pediment is both the oldest and the newest: the marble now there dates from

the extension of the 1950s, but it is an exact replica of the original sandstone. The figures in the tympanum of the pediment are a replication
in white Georgia marble of the original sculpture done between 1825
and 1828 by Luigi Persico, one of the many Italian sculptors hired to
decorate the Capitol. President John Quincy Adams took a personal
interest in the design of this sculpture, eschewing any references to
"heathen mythology" and insisting that the work depict in an "obvious
and intelligent manner" the legislative aims and duties of the nation.
The result is a central figure of America, resting her arm on a shield
and pointing to Justice, who holds scales in one hand and the Constitution in the other. On America's other side, with an eagle between
them, stands Hope. The message conveyed is that Americans should
cultivate justice while striving for success, but, taking no chances, Bulfinch cautioned in a letter, "It is intended that an appropriate inscrip-
tion shall explain the meaning and moral to dull comprehensions."

Responsibility for selecting sculptors to fill the tympanums of the
Senate and House pediments fell to Montgomery Meigs. As supervising
engineer in charge, he had authority to award commissions for everything connected with the construction of the building. By the second
half of the nineteenth century, there were several first-rate American

sculptors from whom to choose, and after careful consideration, Meigs offered the commissions for the Senate and House pediments to Hiram Powers and Thomas Crawford, American sculptors who were living in Italy at the time. Crawford agreed to both the commission and the proffered fee: $20,000 to prepare the full-size models for the House pediment. It was a considerable amount, and Meigs cautioned Crawford in a letter to be discreet, lest Members of Congress get wind of the size of it and start lobbying on behalf of their friends. It was not enough to tempt Powers, however, and when he turned down the invitation, Crawford was asked to do the Senate pediment instead of the House. His sculpture, *Progress of Civilization,* was installed in 1863 and depicts a concept that would be thought offensive today but was not considered so in Crawford's day: the ascendancy of the white race over the Indians. In 1845 John L. O'Sullivan had asserted Americans' "manifest destiny to overspread the continent allotted by Providence," and by the second half of the nineteenth century the concept of "Manifest Destiny" was seldom questioned. Indeed, Crawford's sculpture was so well received that Meigs immediately offered him other highly prized commissions. (Crawford is the only sculptor to be honored with a bust in the Capitol.)

Progress of civilization, IN THE SENATE PEDIMENT, EAST FRONT. THE SCULPTOR, THOMAS CRAWFORD, WANTED TO USE CARRARA MARBLE, BUT MONTGOMERY MEIGS KNEW IT WOULD NOT HOLD UP IN THE WASHINGTON CLIMATE. THE FIGURES WERE MODELED IN ROME BUT CARVED FROM LEE, MASSACHUSETTS, MARBLE. A CENTRAL FIGURE REPRESENTS AMERICA; ON HER LEFT, DEPICTING THE EARLY DAYS OF THE NATION, ARE A WOODSMAN AND A HUNTER, AN INDIAN MOTHER AND CHILD, AND AN INDIAN GRAVE. DEPICTING THE MARCH OF PROGRESS ON HER RIGHT ARE A SOLDIER, A MERCHANT, A MECHANIC, AND A SCHOOLMASTER AND CHILD.

FACING PAGE: THE COLUMBUS DOORS—THE JEWELS OF THE EAST FRONT. EIGHT PANELS CONTAIN SCENES FROM THE LIFE OF COLUMBUS; IN NICHES ON EITHER SIDE OF EACH PANEL ARE STATUES OF HIS FRIENDS, CONTEMPORARIES, AND FELLOW EXPLORERS. ABOVE THESE IS A TYMPANUM SHOWING COLUMBUS LANDING IN THE NEW WORLD, AND CROWNING THE WHOLE ARE A BUST OF COLUMBUS AND AN AMERICAN EAGLE WITH FLAGS. ABOVE: TWO OF THE PANELS SHOW COLUMBUS'S AUDIENCE AT THE COURT OF FERDINAND AND ISABELLA, AND HIS DEPARTURE FROM THE CONVENT OF LA RABIDA. *PAGES 72-73:* THE EAST FRONT AT SUNRISE.

A number of artists vied to be allowed to design the sculpture for the House tympanum, but it was almost half a century before the commission was awarded to Paul Wayland Bartlett, an American living in Paris. The *Apotheosis of Democracy*, in white Georgia marble, was unveiled in 1916.

In front of each of the porticoes on the East Front is a broad staircase leading up to the three main entrances to the building. Under each one is a carriage entrance, covered and convenient, and the preferred means of entry for those who work in the Capitol. The staircases and porticoes, however, are the grand entrances, and Meigs decided that they deserved appropriately imposing doors. He admired the bronze doors produced in Europe, and in the 1850s he awarded commissions for three sets of doors. Crawford was to design those for the Senate and House entrances, which he began doing in 1855. He died in 1857, and his widow asked William H. Rinehart, another American sculptor working in Rome, to complete the work. The two sets of doors are companion pieces, each consisting of six panels and two medallions. The Senate set depicts events in the life of George Washington and the Revolutionary War; the House set portrays scenes from the Revolutionary period.

The doors of the central section are the most magnificent of all. Before the extension of the East Front they opened directly into the Rotunda; now they lead into a vestibule just off of it. They are the work of the young Randolph Rogers, a prolific and highly regarded American sculptor living in Rome and chosen by Meigs. The doors are massive, nearly 17 feet high, and weigh about nine tons. Known as the Columbus Doors, they depict events in the life of the explorer, from the first proposal to the Council of Salamanca of his plan to find a new route to the East, to his death in 1506. The doors were modeled in Rome, cast at the Royal Bavarian Foundry in Munich, and installed between what is now Statuary Hall and the new wing of the House in 1863. It was immediately apparent, however, that doors so magnificent deserved a more prominent display, and in 1871 they were moved to become the principal doors into the Capitol.

For more than a century, two groups of sculpture stood on the cheek blocks on either side of the central steps: *Discovery of America*, by Luigi Persico, and *Rescue*, by Horatio Greenough. Both were controversial from the start. *Discovery* showed Columbus holding a globe, with an Indian girl cowering to the side of him; *Rescue* showed a frontiersman defending his family against a threatening Indian. Even subscribers to

Executed in Bronze
F.v. Miller
Munich 1860

the theory of Manifest Destiny found the sculptures offensive, and in 1939 Congress considered a joint resolution proposing that *Rescue* be "ground into dust and scattered to the four winds, that no more remembrance may be perpetuated of our barbaric past." When the East Front was being extended, it was decided to remove the sculptures permanently. Some time later fate intervened to carry out the resolution: the crane lifting *Rescue* accidentally dropped one of the figures. Today the statue rests in pieces, along with *Discovery,* in storage.

Some of the major events in the country's history are to be read in the works of decorative art and sculpture on the exterior of the Capitol, but every four years the attention of the nation turns instead to history being made there. In 1829 Andrew Jackson became the first President to take the oath of office publicly on the East Front of the Capitol. "Old Hickory," as he was called, had been elected as a man of the people, and he wanted as many of those people as possible to be able to participate in his inauguration. He was not the first President to take the oath of office outdoors; George Washington's first inauguration had taken place on the balcony of Federal Hall in New York, and the venue for James Monroe's first inauguration had to be switched to a specially constructed platform outside the Brick Capitol when it was determined that the building itself was not suitable for the anticipated crowd. Jackson was to begin a tradition: from 1829 until 1977, every elected President except William

Howard Taft would be inaugurated on the East Front of the Capitol. (Taft departed from the tradition in 1909 only because he worried that the blizzard that day might endanger the health of the aging Chief Justice, Melville Weston Fuller, who was to administer the oath.) That tradition was ended and a new one begun in 1981, when Ronald Reagan became the first President to be inaugurated on the West Front. The necessary preparations for an inauguration included building large temporary platforms, and since the East Front is also the main pedestrian and vehicular entrance to the building, the disruption was considerable. The West Front is less used, offers a vast sloping lawn for spectators, and is altogether a more magnificent setting for the ceremony.

Until 1933, inaugurations were held in March. In Washington, this meant that the weather would be unpredictable; the annals are filled with accounts of heavy snow and driving rain. Indeed, weather was to be the undoing of the unfortunate William Henry Harrison, before Ronald Reagan the oldest man ever elected President, and the first to die in

office. Appearing bareheaded at his inauguration in 1841, he caught cold and died thirty days later. In 1933 the Twentieth Amendment to the Constitution was ratified, changing the date for inaugurations to January 20, and making a bad meteorological situation even worse. Yet the weather is never bad enough to deter the thousands of spectators who converge on the Capitol. Sometimes they are rewarded by hearing words uttered that later become part of the heritage of the nation: "We admit of no government by divine right" (William Henry Harrison); "With malice toward none; with charity for all" (Abraham Lincoln); "The only thing we have to fear is fear itself" (Franklin D. Roosevelt); "And so, my fellow Americans, ask not what your country can do for you; ask what you can do for your country" (John F. Kennedy). And they see enacted the ceremony that is the culmination of the democratic process. The Capitol is a worthy stage for such a pageant.

Morning light glances off the pilasters of the senate wing, east front. *Facing page:* under the senate portico, on a late autumn afternoon.

CORRIDORS

OF

POWER

THE CORRIDORS of the Capitol are known by many names, official and unofficial. Some are identified by the artwork or objects in them: the Brumidi Corridors, the Hall of Columns, the Ohio Clock Corridor. Some are nicknamed after the activities carried on there, such as "Gucci Gulch," where lobbyists congregate. Some bear unpoetic but useful designations like East-West Corridor, East Front Hallway, and First Floor Connecting Corridor. Some are dark and narrow, some ornate and grand. Some are merely functional, others are replete with historic significance. ∼ Perhaps nowhere in the Capitol have the philosophical differences be-

tween the Senate and the House been more graphically portrayed than on the corridor walls of their respective wings. Among the Capitol's treasures are the Brumidi Corridors, located on the ground floor of the Senate wing. Constantino Brumidi and his assistants spent more than twenty years producing a visual tribute to milestones in American history, and their work is still ongoing. Spaces that they left unpainted are being filled with scenes they could never have imagined: the Wright brothers' airplane, Lindbergh's *Spirit of St. Louis,* astronauts landing on the moon, and a poignant portrait of the crew of the ill-fated space shuttle *Challenger.*

A DETAIL FROM ONE OF THE PAINTINGS IN THE BRUMIDI CORRIDOR OF THE SENATE WING. *FACING PAGE:* A BUST OF CONSTANTINO BRUMIDI, BY JIMILU MASON, JUST OFF THE BRUMIDI CORRIDOR.

C. BRUMIDI

For years, Members of the House of Representatives neither had nor wanted anything like the Senate corridors. They eschewed any hint of pomp or ceremony and considered unnecessary embellishment to be at odds with Jeffersonian republicanism. Plain brown walls were good enough for them. Some in the Senate dismissed such views as institutional self-contempt; in keeping with their longer term of office, senators tended to take a longer view of things in general. Certainly there were those who disapproved of what they considered to be Brumidi's excessively "European" style, and Walter himself had specified that the walls should be plain and hung with paintings. Nevertheless, decora-

tion of the walls and ceilings of the Senate side of the building proceeded apace and with few apologies.

When the Library of Congress outgrew its quarters in the Capitol and moved into its sumptuous new building across the street in 1897, the spartan appearance of the House wing became even more pronounced by comparison. Members themselves began to feel ashamed when showing constituents around, particularly if their visitors happened to have seen the Library first. In 1901 any remaining scruples were laid aside, and Congress began appropriating money to spruce up the appearance of the House corridors. Joseph Rakeman, working with his

son and assistants, began painting decorations in the corridors, beginning on the second floor outside the House Chamber. In 1970, in anticipation of the nation's Bicentennial, the United States Capitol Historical Society donated money to commission the painter Allyn Cox to begin to decorate the walls and ceilings of the ground floor East-West Corridor on the House side of the building—its answer to the Senate's Brumidi Corridors. Whether it is a worthy answer is up to each individual to judge.

When the Presiding Officer of the Senate officiates in the Senate Chamber, it is theoretically possible for him to look straight ahead and

see the Presiding Officer of the House over in the House Chamber, provided that the doors of both chambers are open and he has phenomenally good eyesight. The two chairs are over 200 yards apart—more than the length of two football fields. Stretching between them is the main corridor of the Capitol.

The central part of this corridor falls within the original Capitol building. The stone floor and walls reflect the young, preindustrial country, reliant upon oxen and brawn for transportation, and building materials that could be obtained within about a forty-mile radius. By the time the extensions were added in the middle of the nineteenth century, steam

power and railroads were employed, and communications had improved to the point where there was one-day mail service between Washington and New York. The corridors of the extensions reflect this progress. Now the builders and decorators of the Capitol had both the financial wherewithal and the logistical means to avail themselves of an array of materials from around the world. Superior marble was brought in not only from Massachusetts, Tennessee, and Vermont, but also from Italy. Ornamental plasterwork began to be used extensively. The floors of both extensions were laid with ceramic encaustic tiles from Minton, Hollins and Company, in Stoke-on-Trent, England. (The Senate is in the process of replacing its worn tiles with new ones made by the same company; the House replaced most of its worn tiles in 1924 with less decorative, more serviceable marble.)

THE STAIRCASE LEADING TO THE SMALL SENATE ROTUNDA, BUILT BY LATROBE AFTER THE FIRE. ITS SITUATION, NEAR WHAT WAS ONCE THE MAIN ENTRANCE TO THE BUILDING, MADE IT ONE OF THE MOST USED STAIRCASES IN THE CAPITOL; IT REMAINS ONE OF THE MOST HANDSOME. *FACING PAGE:* THE GRAND STAIRCASE ON THE EAST SIDE, SENATE WING. A STATUE OF BENJAMIN FRANKLIN BY HIRAM POWERS IS ON THE LOWER LANDING. *PAGES 80-81:* DETAILS OF THE BRUMIDI CORRIDORS, WHERE CLASSICAL GODS AND GODDESSES INTERMINGLE WITH AMERICAN FLORA AND FAUNA. THE FRESCOED LUNETTE, *PAGE 80, CENTER,* IS ENTITLED *SIGNING OF THE FIRST TREATY OF PEACE WITH GREAT BRITAIN.*

Along the length of this principal corridor are several of the most historic areas in the Capitol. The Great Rotunda marks the exact center of the corridor, but on either side of it is a smaller rotunda. That on the House side is one of the oldest rooms in the building, having escaped damage at the hands of the British in 1814. The Small Senate Rotunda, however, is the more beautiful of the two. It is the work of Benjamin Latrobe, and was begun in 1815 in a space that had been the principal stairwell of the Senate wing before the burning of the Capitol. Latrobe relocated the staircase to one side, and rebuilt the rotunda as a primarily functional "ornamental airshaft" to introduce light and ventilation—two important considerations during the early years of the Capitol. For the charming capitals of the sixteen sandstone columns of the colonnade, Latrobe added an American element to the classical Corinthian order. In place of acanthus he used tobacco leaves and flowers, symbolizing the source of wealth of the first American colonies. It was not Latrobe's first flight of fancy. In 1809 he had designed the "corncob" capitals that are found in the old entry vestibule on the floor below. Of these Latrobe wrote that they "obtained . . . more applause from members of Congress than all the works of magnitude or difficulty that surrounded them. They christened them the 'Corn-cob capitals,' whether for the

sake of alliteration I can not tell, but certainly not very appropriately." (Latrobe had a point, but "ears-of-corn capitals" does *not* have the same punch.) They were among the earliest decorative sculptural details in the Capitol, and among the few to escape damage during the fire of 1814.

The southern part of the corridor passes through the center of Statuary Hall, with its collection of the states' favorite sons and daughters, and into the Connecting Corridor, a short hallway that houses some of the overflow statues from the collection. There stands Will Rogers, who quipped: "There's no trick to being a humorist when you have the whole government working for you." As he would have wished, he faces the House Chamber; he always said he wanted to "keep an eye on the boys."

At the southern end of the corridor, outside an office of the House Ways and Means Committee, is an area that was nicknamed "Gucci Gulch" when well-heeled lobbyists congregated there during hearings on the Tax Reform Act of 1986. Lobbyists are as old as the Congress and have long been a fixture in and around the Capitol, in the corridors and in the Rotunda, pleading the causes of the various interests they represent.

On the ground floor of the House wing is the Hall of Columns, another gallery for the statuary given by the states. Here is John Winthrop, complete with breeches and ruff, a sober Puritan and the first governor of the Massachusetts Bay Colony. He distrusted the idea of democracy and thought only those with superior minds, however few they might be, should be entrusted with power. Nearby stands chunky Father Damien, the Martyr of Molokai. The compelling unpretentiousness of the missionary priest from Hawaii, as immortalized by

*D*ETAILS FROM ONE OF THE SENATORS' PRIVATE STAIRCASES —A CHARMING INTERPLAY OF BRONZE CHERUBS, EAGLES, AND DEER. THEY WERE DESIGNED BY BRUMIDI, MODELED BY EDMOND BAUDIN, AND CAST BETWEEN 1857 AND 1859 IN PHILADELPHIA. *FACING PAGE:* THE SMALL SENATE ROTUNDA, WHERE LATROBE INTRODUCED HIS CELEBRATED "TOBACCO" CAPITALS. THE IMPRESSIVE CHANDELIER, OF CZECHOSLO-VAKIAN CRYSTAL, HAS 148 LAMPS AND APPROXIMATELY 14,500 PRISMS. AFTER A CHECK-ERED PAST IN A VAUDEVILLE THEATER AND A CHURCH, IT WAS BOUGHT FOR THE CAPITOL FROM A DEMOLITION COMPANY IN 1965. *PAGES 84-85:* THE OHIO CLOCK CORRIDOR, OUTSIDE THE SENATE CHAMBER, TAKES ITS NAME FROM THE CLOCK THAT WAS FOR YEARS THE OFFICIAL TIMEKEEPER IN THE OLD SENATE CHAMBER. THE SEVENTEEN STARS ON ITS CASE ARE REPUTED TO REPRESENT OHIO'S ENTRY INTO THE UNION AS THE SEVENTEENTH STATE— THE ONLY LINK BETWEEN THE CLOCK AND THE STATE. ONE STAR, HOWEVER, IS SIGNIFI-CANTLY DIFFERENT FROM THE OTHERS, GIVING RISE TO THE RUMOR THAT IT WAS ADDED LATER BY AN OVER-ZEALOUS OHIOAN.

THE RICHLY WROUGHT FAN VAULTING OVER THE EAST DOORWAY INTO THE SENATE CHAMBER IS THE ONLY EXAMPLE OF GOTHIC REVIVAL ARCHITECTURE IN THE CAPITOL. THE DOORS ARE A LUXURIOUS BIRD'S-EYE MAPLE VENEER OVER BAY WOOD MAHOGANY; TO MAKE THE BUILDING LESS VULNERABLE TO FIRE, THE VAULTING AND DOOR FRAMES ARE IRON. *FACING PAGE:* THE CORRIDOR LEADING TO THE EAST STAIRCASE IN THE SENATE WING CONTAINS SEVERAL OF THE BUSTS FROM THE VICE PRESIDENTIAL COLLECTION: AMONG THEM, HUBERT H. HUMPHREY, *LEFT,* AND CHARLES CURTIS, *RIGHT.*

the twentieth-century sculptor Marisol Escobar, sets him apart from his proud bronze and marble colleagues. His statue is also the only piece of contemporary art in the collection.

Like all good landlords, the owners of the Capitol are constantly inspecting their property. During visiting hours on any day of the year, the public areas of the building are crowded with sightseers, and frequently they will be rewarded with the opportunity to glimpse, or even speak to, someone they know well from television or newspapers. It is not in the nature of most congressmen to object to this, but the crowds can make it difficult for them to move about the building. All roads used to lead through the Rotunda, and a chance encounter there with a visiting group from a Member's home district could play havoc with a schedule. A boon for congressmen was the East Front extension of the 1950s, which, in addition to adding two and a half acres of space to the building, created less-traveled north-south corridors for the Members' use. What was formerly the exterior sandstone face of the Capitol is now the inner wall of these corridors; the old windows, no longer admitting light and air, serve more as architectural curiosities.

Even more private are the corridors off which are located the "hide-away" offices of some senior senators. These are the true "corridors of power," and they are kept so studiedly anonymous that the names of the occupants of the offices show up neither on the doors nor on plans of the building.

Members also have private staircases—two in each wing—with magnificent bronze railings and balusters. Everybody else uses the four grand staircases, symmetrically situated on the east and west sides of the Senate and House wings. Designed by Walter, three of the four are made of Tennessee variegated marble, and had Walter had his way, the fourth would have been also. He liked symmetry. But Meigs's belief in variety as the spice of life resulted in one staircase being executed largely in white Italian marble. Over each of the cantilevered staircases is a cast-iron ceiling containing grilles—necessary for the early forced-air ventilation system in the building—and a colorful glass laylight.

On each of the four landings is a large painting. The best known of them, *Westward the Course of Empire Takes Its Way,* was painted by Emanuel Leutze in 1862. It was one of the few works commissioned during the Civil War era, and may well have been a piece of thinly veiled propaganda, intended to glorify, and encourage more people to undertake, the trek westward. A panorama of the Golden Gate—the probable destination—runs along the bottom. It was certainly hoped that it would serve as a sign of confidence in the continuity of government and as a portrayal of the American spirit at a time when that same spirit was being sorely tested.

FACING PAGE: EMANUEL LEUTZE'S *WESTWARD THE COURSE OF EMPIRE TAKES ITS WAY,* IN THE WEST STAIRWAY OF THE HOUSE WING. UNLIKE THE PAINTINGS IN THE THREE OTHER GRAND STAIRWAYS, WHICH WERE PAINTED ON CANVAS, THIS WAS DONE IN A GERMAN MURAL TECHNIQUE KNOWN AS WATER GLASS PAINTING. WATERCOLORS WERE APPLIED DIRECTLY TO THE WALL AND THEN FIXED BY A SPRAY OF WATER GLASS SOLUTION. IT IS A MORE FORGIVING MEDIUM THAN TRUE FRESCO. WHILE BRUMIDI'S WORK WAS BEING CRITICIZED FOR BEING TOO "EUROPEAN," THE GERMAN-BORN LEUTZE WAS SEEN AS HAVING ALL THE CORRECT AMERICAN IDEALS.

TOP: LATROBE'S MUCH-
ADMIRED "CORNCOB" CAPITALS
MAY BE SEEN IN A VESTIBULE
OUTSIDE THE OLD SUPREME
COURT CHAMBER, ALONG
WITH THE BUSTS OF THADDEUS
KOSCIUSZKO, *LEFT,* GIUSEPPE
GARIBALDI, *CENTER,* AND K. K.
(CASIMIR) PULASKI, *RIGHT.*

LEFT: A STATUE OF JOHN PETER
GABRIEL MUHLENBERG BY
BLANCHE NEVIN, IN THE SMALL
HOUSE ROTUNDA. *RIGHT:* A
WALL DETAIL WITH SNAKES,
CORN, AND DOLPHINS, FROM
THE NORTH-SOUTH CORRIDOR,
EAST SIDE. *FACING PAGE:* THE
ORNATE PLASTERWORK IN THE
CORRIDOR—DEPICTING FLORA
AND FAUNA—IS BY ERNEST
THOMAS. ON THE HOUSE SIDE,
THE MINTON TILES THAT ORIG-
INALLY COVERED THE FLOORS
WERE TAKEN UP AND REPLACED
WITH MARBLE IN THE 1920S.

BENEATH THE DOME

THE BUILDERS of the Capitol turned their attention to the central section last because it was the least essential part of the building. The Senate and the House needed rooms in which to carry on the business of government, but from the beginning the central section was more of an architectural necessity than a practical one. It fell to Bulfinch to finish it, and in doing so, he at long last completed the most prominent feature of Thornton's plan, the domed rotunda. It was based on the Pantheon in Rome, one of Jefferson's favorite buildings, and its perfect proportions—96 feet in diameter and 96 feet high—replicated those of the Pantheon, albeit on a slightly smaller scale.

The Rotunda was always intended to be the ceremonial heart of the building. While the Senate and the House controlled their respective wings, however, the Rotunda was a kind of no-man's-land, coming under the authority of neither of them. And since no one was directly responsible for what happened there, an amazing variety of things did. Soon after it was finished in 1824, vendors set up stalls in it, selling everything from silks and birdcages to shovels and machinery. It was a prime location because constituents who came to see their congressmen used the Rotunda as a waiting room. Artists hoping for government commissions set up exhibits of their work where congressmen

THE DECLARATION OF INDE-
PENDENCE, AT INDEPENDENCE
HALL, PHILADELPHIA, BY JOHN
TRUMBULL, IN THE ROTUNDA.
FACING PAGE: LOOKING INTO
THE DOME TOWARD BRUMIDI'S
FRIEZE AND THE APOTHEOSIS
OF WASHINGTON.

could not help but see them. One Member described the area as a collection of "pictures and butter churns, cannons and busts, basso
relievos and statues promiscuously blended." It was even available for
hire, there being few public rooms of its size in Washington.

Yet these were simply growing pains. The Rotunda was being decorated with sculptures and paintings—some of the most important in
the Capitol—and was evolving into what it would eventually become: a
breathtaking ceremonial room for many of the nation's most joyful and
most solemn events.

The first official ceremony to take place there was a reception in 1824
for the aging Marquis de Lafayette, who, in grateful recognition of his
support for the revolutionary cause, had been invited by the government to pay a state visit to the United States. In 1835 the Rotunda was
the scene of an assassination attempt against Andrew Jackson. A man
who maintained he was the heir to the British throne tried to shoot the
President, whom he blamed—illogically, in light of his claimed lin-
eage—for his inability to get a job. His pistols misfired, and he was
later judged to be insane.

In 1852 Henry Clay of Kentucky, a former Speaker of the House who
brought brilliant gifts of oratory to both chambers, became the first person to be accorded the honor of lying in state in the Rotunda. In 1865 a
black-draped catafalque bore the remains of Abraham Lincoln. Since

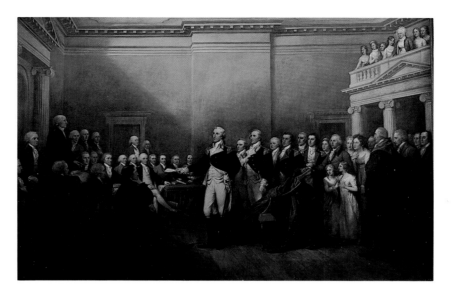

then, those honored on the same catafalque have included the other assassinated Presidents as well as several other Presidents. Pierre L'Enfant, unknown soldiers of the four wars the country has fought during this century, and a number of Senate and House Members have also lain in state in the Rotunda, the place where the nation pays its last respects.

On happier occasions the Rotunda is the scene for dedication ceremonies for works of art and for other events as authorized by Congress. A historic precedent was set in 1985 when bitter cold prevented President Reagan's second inauguration from taking place outside on the West Front; he took the oath of office in the Rotunda instead.

Bulfinch's Rotunda can easily be visualized today. Gone is the original low dome, but everything else, up to a height of 48 feet, is his. Fluted Doric pilasters embellish the curving sandstone walls. Above each of the four entrance doors are panels carved in relief, showing scenes from early American colonial history. Indians are portrayed in all four, not always sympathetically. Also on the walls are busts of four explorers: John Cabot, Christopher Columbus, Sir Walter Raleigh, and Sieur de La Salle. Most interesting of all, however, are the eight large historical paintings, and particularly the four by John Trumbull. These, the first federally commissioned paintings (1817), show scenes from the Revolutionary

TWO OF THE EIGHT LARGE HISTORICAL PAINTINGS IN THE ROTUNDA. *TOP:* JOHN TRUMBULL'S *GENERAL GEORGE WASHINGTON RESIGNING HIS COMMISSION TO CONGRESS AS COMMANDER IN CHIEF OF THE ARMY AT ANNAPOLIS, MARYLAND, DECEMBER 23RD, 1783.* ALTHOUGH TRUMBULL'S WORK IS PARTICULARLY VALUABLE BECAUSE OF ITS HISTORICAL AUTHENTICITY, HE WAS NOT ABOVE TAKING ARTISTIC LICENSE WHEN THE OCCASION DEMANDED. HERE A FOND MARTHA IS SHOWN WATCHING THE PROCEEDINGS FROM A BALCONY. IN FACT, MARTHA WAS AT MOUNT VERNON AT THE TIME. *BELOW:* THE LAST OF THE EIGHT PAINTINGS COMMISSIONED FOR THE ROTUNDA WAS INSTALLED IN 1855. THE FIRST ARTIST TO RECEIVE THE COMMISSION DIED BEFORE COMPLETING HIS PAINTING, AND FRIENDS OF SAMUEL MORSE LOBBIED UNSUCCESSFULLY FOR HIM TO BE ALLOWED TO FINISH IT. BUT MEMBERS HAD NOT LIKED ANY OF THE SEVEN PAINTINGS THEY HAD ALREADY SEEN, AND THERE WAS LITTLE URGENCY ATTACHED TO COMPLETING THE PROJECT. A NEW COMMISSION FOR THE EIGHTH EVENTUALLY WENT TO WILLIAM H. POWELL, WHO PAINTED *DISCOVERY OF THE MISSISSIPPI BY DE SOTO, A.D. 1541,* IN 1853.

Left: A BRONZE STATUE OF
GEORGE WASHINGTON, IN THE
UNIFORM OF COMMANDER-IN-
CHIEF OF THE AMERICAN ARMY,

BY FRENCH SCULPTOR JEAN-
ANTOINE HOUDON. THE ORIGI-
NAL MARBLE FROM WHICH
THIS STATUE WAS CAST WAS
SCULPTED FROM LIFE IN 1788;
IT IS IN RICHMOND, VIRGINIA.
RIGHT: HEAD OF A STATUE
OF JEFFERSON BY P. J. DAVID
D'ANGERS. PERIPATETIC IN LIFE
AND IN BRONZE, THIS JEFFER-
SON STOOD BRIEFLY IN THE
ROTUNDA AND THEN FOR MANY
YEARS IN FRONT OF THE WHITE
HOUSE. IN 1874 THE STATUE
WAS RETURNED TO THE CAPI-
TOL AND, FINALLY, TO ITS HOME
IN THE ROTUNDA.

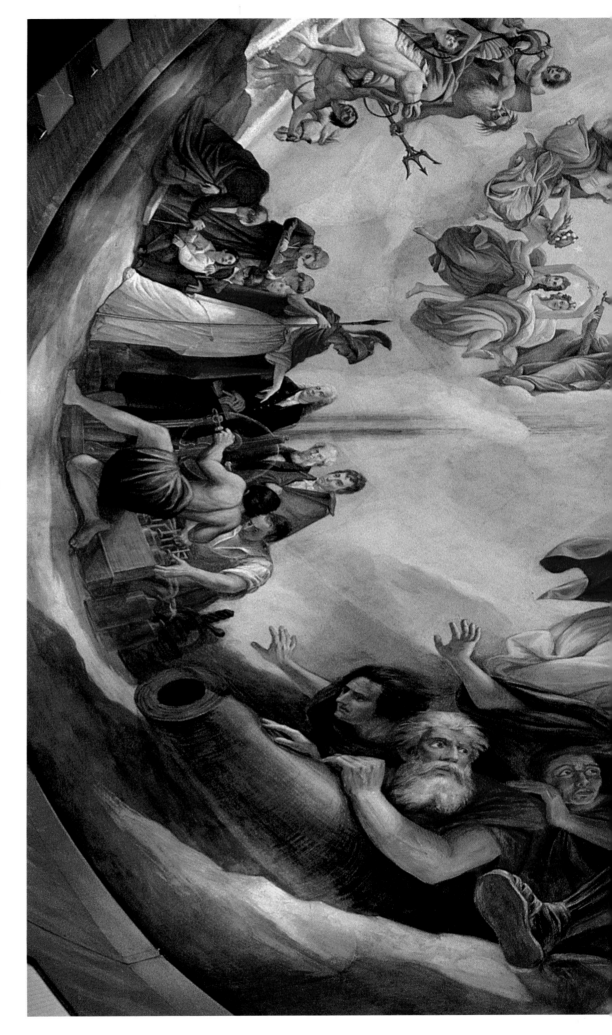

Brumidi's *THE APOTHEOSIS OF WASHINGTON* SHOWS WASHINGTON SEATED IN HEAVEN WITH THE FIGURE OF LIBERTY ON ONE SIDE, VICTORY AND FAME ON THE OTHER. THIRTEEN MAIDENS, REPRESENTING THE THIRTEEN ORIGINAL STATES, WAFT IN A CIRCLE AROUND HIM, HOLDING ALOFT A BANNER WITH THE WORDS *E PLURIBUS UNUM.* DIRECTLY BENEATH WASHINGTON IS ARMED LIBERTY TRAMPLING TYRANNY AND KINGLY POWER; LIBERTY'S FACE IS SUPPOSEDLY THAT OF BRUMIDI'S YOUNG WIFE, LOLA GERMON. AROUND THE PERIMETER ARE SIX GROUPS REPRESENTING WAR, ART AND SCIENCES, MARINE, COMMERCE, MECHANICS, AND AGRICULTURE.

War period. They are all the more valuable because Trumbull, who was George Washington's aide-de-camp during the first year of the Revolutionary War, had been present at some of the events he depicted. He subsequently studied painting in the United States and Europe with the express intention of recording what he had seen. In seeking the commission for the paintings, Trumbull was perhaps excessively modest: "Future artists may arise with far Superior Talents, but time has already withdrawn almost all their Models; and I . . . was one of the youngest Actors in the early scenes of the War." He knew many of the individuals he painted; a number of them, including George Washington, actually sat for him at one time or another, in the interest of historical accuracy. It was at Trumbull's urging that the hole that had been left in the floor of the Rotunda, through which future beholders were to gaze on a monument to George Washington in the Crypt below, was closed up. He complained that damp air rising through it was producing mold on his paintings. In any case, no monument was ever erected there. Congress, moved by sorrow at the time of Washington's death, had devised a grand scheme for a memorial, but thirty years later there were more reasons not to build it than to build it.

A frieze with laurel leaves surmounts the pilasters of the Rotunda, and marks the extent of Bulfinch's design; everything above the frieze was added when Walter designed the new dome. Had not fate inter-

vened, all the painting in the new dome might have been the
work of one man—"the Michelangelo of the Capitol," as Brumidi came to be called. He finished painting the fresco in the
canopy of the dome, but only partially completed the frieze
around the collar of the dome. This was plagued with misfortune
from the start. Meigs originally had intended Crawford to execute a series of high-relief sculptures along it, but Crawford died
while it was still being planned. In 1877 Brumidi was commissioned to do the work in fresco, using a monochrome palette of
whites and browns in order to achieve a sculptural effect. It was
while working on this that Brumidi almost fell from his scaffold
and died a few months later. Filippo Costaggini carried on,
working from Brumidi's designs, but when he had used all the
sketches that Brumidi had left, a 30-foot gap remained unfilled.
It remained incomplete until 1950, when Congress authorized
Allyn Cox to paint scenes depicting the Civil War, the Spanish-
American War, and the Birth of Aviation. Costaggini was able to leave
his mark, however. In a tree trunk near the section showing the Death
of Tecumseh he painted a face—possibly his own.

In the canopy of the dome is Brumidi's allegorical masterwork, *The
Apotheosis of George Washington,* painted in true fresco in eleven
months and unveiled in 1866. Covering an area of 4,664 square feet, it
depicts the glorification of Washington. A nineteenth-century visitor,
S. D. Wyeth, described its effect: "The great fresco picture by Brumidi
arrests the gaze as though the sky had opened." The climb to the top of
the dome is off limits now, except by special permission. The ascent is
by 183 steps that thread their way up, eerily and precariously, between
the inner and outer shells of the dome, to emerge on the narrow exte-

Top: ALEXANDER HAMILTON, BY
HORATIO STONE. *BOTTOM:*
ULYSSES S. GRANT, BY FRANKLIN
SIMMONS—A GIFT FROM THE
GRAND ARMY OF THE REPUBLIC
IN 1890.

rior balcony at the foot of the colonnade just
below the Statue of Freedom, affording a spectacular, wind-whipped view. Or, a few steps lower,
one can stand under the canopy of the dome and
marvel at the scale and detail of the figures in
Brumidi's fresco.

The statues and busts in the Rotunda are pre-
dominantly those of Presidents. A statue of Jefferson done in 1833 by the French sculptor P. J.
David d'Angers is considered by some to be the
most important work of art in the Capitol. The
first statue to be placed there, it was the gift of
Uriah P. Levy, an admirer of Jefferson's views on
religious freedom. Two busts in the Rotunda—of
George Washington and General Lafayette—are

*J*OHN TRUMBULL HOPED TO DO
ALL EIGHT OF THE LARGE HIS-
TORICAL PAINTINGS PLANNED
FOR THE ROTUNDA. HE HAD
COMPLETED SKETCHES FOR
THEM (NOW AT YALE UNIVER-
SITY), BUT HIS FIRST FOUR
WERE SO HARSHLY CRITICIZED
THAT HE WAS NOT ASKED TO
CONTINUE, AND FOR NEARLY
TWENTY YEARS CONGRESS DE-
CLINED TO AWARD COMMIS-
SIONS FOR THE REMAINING
FOUR PANELS. REPRESENTATIVE
JOHN RANDOLPH OF VIRGINIA
CLAIMED HE COULD NOT WALK
THROUGH THE ROTUNDA WITH-
OUT FEELING "ASHAMED OF
THE STATE OF THE ARTS" IN
AMERICA. COMMISSIONS EVEN-
TUALLY WERE GIVEN TO FOUR
AMERICAN ARTISTS, AND
THREE OF THEIR PAINTINGS
WERE INSTALLED IN THE 1840S.
TOP: ROBERT W. WEIR'S *THE
EMBARKATION OF THE PILGRIMS
AT DELFT HAVEN, HOLLAND,
JULY 22ND, 1620,* SHOWS MILES
STANDISH KNEELING AT RIGHT.
BOTTOM: JOHN G. CHAPMAN'S
*BAPTISM OF POCAHONTAS AT
JAMESTOWN, VIRGINIA, 1613.*
POCAHONTAS IS DEPICTED IN
TWO OTHER PLACES IN THE
ROTUNDA, AND WAS SEEN BY
SOME TO REPRESENT THE
IDEAL NATIVE AMERICAN: SHE
WAS BAPTIZED A CHRISTIAN
(WITH THE BLESSING OF HER
FAMILY, SHOWN BEHIND HER);
SHE MARRIED THE ENGLISH-
MAN JOHN ROLFE; AND SHE
ACTED AS A FAITHFUL LIAISON
BETWEEN HER PEOPLE AND
THE COLONISTS.

also the work of David d'Angers; both replace ones destroyed in the 1851 Library of Congress fire. That of Washington was the gift of the French nation, and a descendant of General Lafayette contributed to its purchase. A bronze statue of George Washington is noteworthy for being cast from the only statue of Washington sculpted while he was alive. Jean-Antoine Houdon, a French sculptor chosen by Jefferson and Franklin, visited Mount Vernon to observe and take measurements of the 54-year-old general. A statue of Lincoln is the work of Vinnie Ream, who was only 17 years old when she asked for a chance to sculpt the President. Despite her conspicuous talents, her request went largely ignored until Lincoln learned that she was *poor.* He at once allowed her into the White House and gave her all the access she needed, during what were to be the last five months of his life. She was the first woman artist to be given a government commission.

Also on display in the Rotunda is an exact reproduction in silver-gilt of the Magna Carta, the great statement of civil liberties that King John of England was forced to sign in 1215, and which was the well-spring of many of the aspirations of the American Revolution. It was a gift from the British Parliament on the occasion of the bicentennial of that revolution.

A recent acquisition in the Rotunda is a bust of Dr. Martin Luther King, Jr., sculpted by John Wilson and dedicated in 1986. It was commissioned by Congress to honor a man who "used the ideals of Christ and the methods of Mahatma Gandhi," and who, for many Americans, symbolizes the equality of all Americans.

Carl Sandburg described the Rotunda as standing "midway between the House and Senate chambers, midway between those seats and aisles of heartbreak and passion." The work of government takes place at both ends of the building, but the symbolic heart of the Capitol is the Rotunda, that soaring political cathedral in which all the diversities and conflicts, all the "heartbreak and passion," are forgotten—for a moment, at least—in the contemplation of something loftier.

GRAND THEATERS

OF AN

EARLIER AGE

THREE HISTORIC ROOMS in the Capitol have been designated as museum rooms. All three are the work of Benjamin Henry Latrobe, to whom fell the responsibility for designing most of the interior spaces within Thornton's original plan. The two rooms on the Senate side, the Old Supreme Court Chamber and the Old Senate Chamber directly above it, have been faithfully restored to their mid-nineteenth-century appearance, and on the House side, the old Hall of Representatives was adapted in 1864 to become Statuary Hall. ∽ The Old Supreme Court Chamber, on the ground floor of the original north wing, is in the same location as

the room in which the Senate first met in 1800. ∽ The Hall for the House of Representatives, which Latrobe completed in 1807, was described by some as the most beautiful room in America, and compared with it, the Senate's cheerless and cramped ground-floor chamber appeared to great disadvantage. Moreover, the Senate met on a lower floor than the House, which seemed symbolically inappropriate. Add to this the fact that the Senate wing was already in a poor state of repair, despite its relative newness, and there was more than enough justification for Latrobe to undertake a major rebuilding. In 1808 he began work on a plan to

A CORINTHIAN CAPITAL
FROM A COLUMN IN STATUARY
HALL. *FACING PAGE:* THE OLD
SENATE CHAMBER, DESIGNED
BY BENJAMIN HENRY LATROBE.

$\mathcal{A}$ BUST OF JOHN MARSHALL, CHIEF JUSTICE OF THE UNITED STATES (1801–1835), BY HIRAM POWERS. BUSTS OF THE CHIEF JUSTICES WERE COMMISSIONED BEGINNING IN THE 1830S; THOSE OF THE FIRST FIVE MEN TO PRESIDE OVER THE COURT—JOHN JAY, JOHN RUTLEDGE, OLIVER ELLSWORTH, JOHN MARSHALL, AND ROGER B. TANEY—ARE DISPLAYED IN THE OLD SUPREME COURT CHAMBER; THOSE OF LATER CHIEF JUSTICES ARE IN THE SUPREME COURT BUILDING.

construct a larger and worthier two-story room for the Senate on the floor above, and a one-story room on the floor below for the Supreme Court, which had hitherto been meeting in a "meanly furnished and very inconvenient" committee room elsewhere in the building. In 1810 the work was completed; the Senate moved upstairs and the Court took up residence underneath.

For the Supreme Court Chamber, Latrobe designed a vaulted space of ambitious proportions, "one of the most extraordinary ever attempted as to *span* and *altitude*," but one that, it will be recalled, had already exacted a tragic cost in the collapse of an arch during construction. The chamber was built with such "uncommon solidarity" that, despite the best efforts of the British, it was damaged but not entirely destroyed in the fire of 1814. In reconstructing the room after the fire, Latrobe finally achieved what he had long sought: complete harmony between architectural and engineering elements. The room was hailed immediately as a triumph. Its unusual lobed ceiling was intersected by structural ribs, which observers described as an "umbrella vault," or "half a pumpkin shell." A triple archway supported by sturdy Doric columns ran along the east wall; within the arches were windows that, before the East Front was extended, opened to the outside. The Supreme Court justices had a tradition of fortifying themselves with the best Madeira they could find whenever it rained; legend has it that Chief Justice John Marshall, a strong proponent of the supremacy of the nation's highest court, would look out of those windows on a fine day, remind his colleagues of their national jurisdiction, and suggest that *somewhere* in the nation it must be raining at that moment.

During the fifty years in which the Court met there, the chamber was the scene of some remarkable arguments and oratory, and it became a popular social gathering point. Foremost among those whose reputations were made there was Daniel Webster, and the chamber was always crowded with spectators whenever he was to argue a case.

The Supreme Court continued to meet in this chamber until 1860, by which time the Senate had moved again, into its new chamber in the newly completed extension. Once again the Justices followed along behind, settling contentedly into the room the senators had just vacated. The critical acclaim their old chamber had garnered was one thing; on a practical level it had proved to be cold, damp, and dark. Indeed, a plaster relief of Justice, sculpted by Carlo Franzoni after the fire of 1814, shows that mythical figure without her traditional blindfold; it was remarked that the room was too dark for her to see anyway!

The chamber was refitted as the Court's Law Library and served as such until the Supreme Court moved out of the building in 1935. It then became the Congressional Law Library until 1950, when it suffered the indignity of being divided into four rooms for the Joint Committee on Atomic Energy, and, eventually, being used for storage.

In anticipation of the nation's Bicentennial celebration in 1976, the room was restored as faithfully as possible to its mid-nineteenth-century appearance, using contemporary descriptions and an 1854 floor plan. Such painstaking restoration of the oldest part of the Capitol is evidence of the nation's respect for the earliest days of its history, and for the momentous decisions and debates that took place in this room.

Directly above the Old Supreme Court Chamber stands the Old Senate Chamber, which the Senate first occupied in 1810. The Senate's first decade in its new home was not auspicious. Four years after the senators moved there they were forced out when the British burned the building. In 1815 Latrobe began the work of restoration, but he resigned in 1817 and the completion of his design fell to his successor, Charles Bulfinch. Not until December 1819 would the chamber be ready for the Senate to return.

The room was meticulously restored for the Bicentennial, and today shows how brilliantly Latrobe succeeded in creating a fitting stage for the dramatic events that would mark the Senate's nearly fifty-year occupancy of the room. The semicircular shape of the room was suggested by the Greek theaters Jefferson so admired; the eight columns along the east wall were inspired by the columns of the Erechtheion in Athens. The desk of the vice president, who serves as president of the Senate, sits on a raised platform under an ornate canopy draped in crimson fabric and surmounted by a gilt eagle with a shield. The desk and the eagle and shield are original pieces. Pride of place in the Old Senate Chamber is given to the "porthole" portrait of George Washington painted by Rembrandt Peale; it hangs in the center of the east wall, directly above the vice president's desk, and is one of the most important works of art in the Capitol. Behind the vice president's desk is a loggia where senators used to congregate before they had offices of their own. Natural lighting for the room came from windows on the east wall and from six skylights in the ceiling. Additional lighting was provided by a chandelier and lamps fueled by oil and, later, by gas.

Facing the vice president's dais, in rising tiers, are reproductions of the desks of the sixty-four men who comprised the Senate when it last occupied the room. A

*B*UST OF THE FIFTH CHIEF JUSTICE, ROGER B. TANEY, BY AUGUSTUS SAINT-GAUDENS, IN THE ROBING ROOM OF THE OLD SUPREME COURT CHAMBER. *PAGES 110-111:* THE OLD SUPREME COURT CHAMBER, WITH ITS CHARACTERISTIC "UMBRELLA" VAULTING, APPEARS MUCH AS IT DID IN THE MID-NINETEENTH CENTURY. ABOUT A THIRD OF THE FURNISHINGS ARE ORIGINAL PIECES, INCLUDING SEVEN OF THE NINE JUSTICES' DESKS. WHERE THE ORIGINAL PIECES WERE NOT AVAILABLE, EXACT REPRODUCTIONS WERE MADE. THE CARPET WAS COPIED FROM ONE THAT APPEARS IN A PORTRAIT OF JOHN MARSHALL.

central aisle runs down the middle, dividing the desks evenly and not along party lines, as would become the custom in the latter part of the nineteenth century.

In the earliest years of its history, the Senate, unlike the House, conducted its affairs behind closed doors, but in 1795, in response to public pressure, the first Senate gallery was opened. In his original plan for the chamber Latrobe accordingly placed a small public gallery behind the vice president's dais. The Senate's proceedings proved to be so popular an entertainment that a second gallery was added along the same wall when the chamber was reconstructed after the fire. This too proved inadequate, and it also blocked light and air from the windows, so in 1828 Charles Bulfinch removed the upper gallery and added instead a sweeping semicircular balcony around the entire back of the chamber. On days when that failed to accommodate visitors, senators chivalrously relinquished their own seats on the floor to the ladies.

From those who occupied the galleries have come a wealth of telling—and sometimes humorous—eyewitness accounts of the events taking place on the floor of the Senate. In 1835 Alexis de Tocqueville wrote admiringly: "The Senate is composed of eloquent advocates,

distinguished generals, wise magistrates, and statesmen of note, whose arguments would do honor to the most remarkable parliamentary debates of Europe." (The French aristocrat was far less complimentary about the members of the House of Representatives, whom he dismissed as "almost all obscure individuals . . . village lawyers, men in trade, or even persons belonging to the lower classes of society.")

THE OLD SENATE CHAMBER, IN WHICH THE SENATE MET FROM 1810 TO 1859, WAS RESTORED IN THE 1970S BY THE SENATE COMMISSION ON ART AND ANTIQUITIES TO LOOK MUCH AS IT DID DURING THE GOLDEN AGE OF THE SENATE. AMONG THE ORIG-

Frances Trollope wrote that although the senators looked like gentlemen, "I would I could add they do not spit." Edgar Allan Poe echoed her feelings: "If I were to drop my wallet on the floor of the Senate, I would not retrieve it without a gloved hand." Margaret Bayard Smith, a Washington doyenne, summed up the attraction of the gallery: "A debate on any political principle would have had no such attraction. But personalities are irresistible. It is a kind of moral gladiatorship. . . . The Senate Chamber . . . is the present arena and never were the amphitheatres of Rome more crowded . . ."

The personalities *were* irresistible. The second quarter of the nineteenth century has been called the Golden Age of the Senate, when the art of oratory in the United States Congress reached heights that have never been surpassed. For much of that time, the "great triumvirate"—

INAL FURNISHINGS ARE THE CURVED DESK AT WHICH THE VICE PRESIDENT SAT, *FACING PAGE*, AND THE FINE GILT EAGLE AND SHIELD, DATING FROM THE 1820S, ABOVE THE PODIUM, *LEFT.* THE SILK DAMASK SWAGS AND CURTAINS, *RIGHT*, SUSPENDED FROM A HANDSOMELY CARVED BALDACHINO, WERE COPIED FROM A FABRIC USED IN THE ORIGINAL CHAMBER.

THE ELABORATELY COFFERED
HALF-DOME CEILING OF THE
OLD SENATE CHAMBER. THE
SIX SKYLIGHTS ORIGINALLY
PROVIDED NATURAL LIGHTING
FOR THE ROOM; ADDITIONAL
LIGHT CAME FROM A CHANDE-
LIER AND LAMPS. THE BUNDLED
ARROWS IN THE CEILING MOLD-
INGS SYMBOLIZE STRENGTH
THROUGH UNITY.

John C. Calhoun of South Carolina, Henry Clay of Kentucky, and Daniel Webster of Massachusetts—held center stage on the Senate floor. The debate over slavery and the preservation of the Union dominated all else, and the passions that it aroused on both sides found eloquent and dramatic expression in the speeches of these three inveterate rivals. Calhoun was thought by many, including Webster, to possess the most brilliant intellect in the government. Webster's thundering delivery could hold the packed galleries spellbound for hours at a time. And Clay, the Great Compromiser, was a skillful extemporaneous speaker who reveled in the art of debate. The three men disagreed fundamentally and violently; Calhoun and Clay would go for years without speaking, except on the Senate floor. Yet their respect for each other's integrity and patriotism appears to have been boundless. When Clay left the Senate in 1842, Calhoun embraced him with tears streaming down his face. He later remarked: "I don't like Clay. He is a bad man, an imposter, a creature of wicked schemes. I won't speak to him, but, by God, I love him!" Clay for his part grieved at Calhoun's death: "No more shall we behold that torrent of clear, concise, compact logic, poured out from his lips, which, if it did not always carry conviction to our judgment, commanded our great admiration." Webster, too, paid Calhoun generous tribute: "We shall carry with us a deep sense of his honor and integrity, his amiable deportment in life, and the purity of his exalted patriotism." Both Clay and Webster were pallbearers at his funeral.

The culmination for the "great triumvirate" came during the Compromise of 1850, perhaps the most important debate of the century. Clay came out of retirement in a desperate attempt to effect a compromise and avert the dissolution of the Union, which he correctly saw would make civil war inevitable. He sought and secured Webster's support, support that would be seen as betrayal by abolitionists and would cost Webster any hope of attaining his own Presidential ambitions. On March 7, 1850, Webster addressed a chamber crammed to capacity:

Mr. President—I wish to speak today not as a Massachusetts man, nor as a Northern man, but as an American, and a member of the Senate of the United States. . . . I have a part to act, not for my own security and safety, for I am looking out for no fragment upon which to float away from the wreck, if wreck there must be, but for the good of the whole, and the preservation of all. . . . I speak today for the preservation of the Union: Hear me for my cause.

Calhoun, gaunt and dying, was carried into the chamber to hear the speech. By the end of the month he was dead, and within two years Clay and Webster had followed him. None of them would know that their heroic efforts to stave off the fraternal bloodshed they so dreaded would ultimately fail. With their deaths began the decline of the Golden Age of the Senate.

In 1859 the Senate's new chamber in the recently completed extension was ready, and in one of their last acts of unity before the Civil War, the senators marched in procession to their new home. In quitting the Old Senate Chamber, Senator John J. Crittenden paid tribute to it:

> Here questions of American constitutions and laws have been debated; questions of peace and war have been debated and decided; questions of empire have occupied the attention of this assemblage in times past; this was the grand theater upon which these things have been enacted. They give a sort of consecrated character to this Hall.

The third museum room in the Capitol is Statuary Hall, formerly the Hall of the House, where the House of Representatives met from 1807 until 1857.

Latrobe's original chamber for the House of Representatives had been destroyed in the fire of 1814. It had borne the imprint of the architect's sometime patron, sometime irritant, Thomas Jefferson. Jefferson had agreed to Latrobe's idea to alter the room's plan from an ellipse to two semicircles joined by a rectangle—an easier thing to construct. But Jefferson had insisted on Corinthian columns around the perimeter of the room, modeled after the Temple of the Winds in Athens, when Latrobe's preference was for the Doric order. Jefferson also, it will be recalled, had forced Latrobe to install one hundred skylights in the ceiling, against the latter's better judgment. Occasionally Jefferson's peremptory manner got the better of Latrobe and the architect would need to vent his frustration, as he did in a letter he wrote to his Clerk of the Works, John Lenthall:

> . . . You and I are both blockheads. Presidents and Vice Presidents are the only architects and poets, and prophets for aught I know in the United States. Therefore let us fall down and worship them . . .

THE FAMOUS "PORTHOLE" PORTRAIT OF GEORGE WASHINGTON BY REMBRANDT PEALE, IN THE OLD SENATE CHAMBER. PAINTED IN 1823, THE PORTRAIT WAS PURCHASED BY THE SENATE FOR $2,000 IN 1832— THE CENTENNIAL OF WASHINGTON'S BIRTH. REMBRANDT PEALE HAD PAINTED WASHINGTON FROM LIFE, AND IT WAS SAID BY THOSE WHO KNEW WASHINGTON THAT THIS PORTRAIT CAPTURED THE MAN BETTER THAN ANY OTHER. PEALE HIMSELF HOPED IT WOULD COME TO BE SEEN AS THE "STANDARD LIKENESS" OF THE FIRST PRESIDENT.

But as political meddling goes, Jefferson's was unusually benign, and often constructive. And when all was said and done, Jefferson had praised Latrobe generously, saying he was the only man in America capable of having designed so splendid a room.

In rebuilding the room after the fire, Latrobe created a handsome semicircular chamber (his preference from the beginning) that is one of America's earliest examples of Greek Revival architecture. He designed columns as he wanted them, of breccia marble with capitals of Italian marble, based on the Choragic Monument of Lysicrates.

There had been one serious problem with the earlier room, and John Randolph of Virginia put his finger on it when he described it as "handsome and fit for anything but the use intended." Due to a parabolic reflection caused by the curved ceiling of the room, the acoustics were terrible. The acoustics in the rebuilt room were, if anything, even worse. The curved ceiling, painted only to *look* coffered, was as efficient a sounding board as could be devised. Every conceivable remedy was tried: curtains were hung, a curved wooden wall was erected behind the columns, and false ceilings of silk and canvas were installed. Bulfinch even designed a flat iron-and-glass ceiling (the curvature of the existing one had been identified as the problem), but it was never installed. The bedeviled Members sought advice from every quarter, including Thornton, who could not resist pointing out that they would not have

The elegantly curved ceiling of Statuary Hall—formerly the Hall of the House—was a bane to those who tried to hear and be heard in the hall beneath it. *FACING PAGE:* THE former Hall of the House of Representatives now houses about one-third of the National Statuary Hall collection. In the foreground, holding a cross aloft, is Father Junipero Serra, a Franciscan friar who, despite his advanced age and deteriorating health, established nine missions in California before his death in Monterey in 1784.

had the problem had they kept to his original plan. What is demonstrated to tourists today as a curious echo effect was a continuing and intolerable nuisance to Members trying to hear and be heard in the chamber. John Quincy Adams once stopped in midspeech, refusing to continue as long as "this gentleman in my rear" kept repeating his words. The problem was solved only when the House moved to its new chamber in 1857.

For seven years after the House moved the room languished in a deplorable state, with no consensus on what should be done with it. The possibility of turning it into an art gallery was raised, but the disposition of columns and lack of wall space argued against it. There are reports that vendors moved in, selling everything from mousetraps to chickens, root beer to tobacco, and causing embarrassment to Members who had to walk through a virtual market on the way to the House Chamber. Before long it succumbed to that occupational hazard of rooms in the Capitol that are temporarily without a specific purpose: it became a storage area.

In 1864 Representative Justin Morrill of Vermont proposed the perfect solution: to create a National Statuary Hall. Congress passed an Act inviting each state to provide up to two statues, in marble or bronze, of deceased persons whom they considered worthy of national commemoration. By 1933 sixty-five statues had been received, and Statuary Hall was beginning to look as congested as it had during some of the House's more riveting debates. Moreover, there was concern about the ability of the floor to support such weight. Since then, some of the statues have been moved to other suitable locations in the Capitol. There are now ninety-five statues in the collection; five states have not yet decided who their second worthy should be, but since there is no deadline—and all selections are final—they are wise to take their time.

Five Presidents were inaugurated in this room: James Madison, James Monroe, John Quincy Adams, Andrew Jackson, and Millard Fillmore. Adams, who returned to serve in the House for seventeen years after his term as President, suffered a fatal stroke at his desk here in 1848. He died two days later in a nearby room and was eulogized by Senator Thomas Hart Benton: "Where could death have found him but at the post of duty?" A bronze plaque marks the spot where his desk stood. Plaques in the floor also commemorate the seven other members of the House who served in this room before going on to become President.

Two pieces of sculpture in Statuary Hall are among the oldest in the Capitol. They were commissioned for the Hall when it was being rebuilt after the fire and are the work of two of the Italian sculptors who

FIRST KING
OF
ALL HAWAII

UNITED THE ISLAND
CHIEFDOMS INTO A
PEACEFUL KINGDOM

C1758–1819

THE PLASTER STATUE OF *LIBERTY AND THE EAGLE*, BY ENRICO CAUSICI, WAS PLACED IN STATUARY HALL SHORTLY AFTER THE FIRE OF 1814; IT MAY BE THE EARLIEST EXTANT REPRESENTATION OF LIBERTY IN THE UNITED STATES. CAUSICI DIED BEFORE HE COULD EXECUTE THE STATUE IN MARBLE. LIBERTY HOLDS THE CONSTITUTION; TO HER LEFT IS A SERPENT, SYMBOL OF WISDOM. ON THE FRIEZE BELOW IS AN EAGLE CARVED IN SANDSTONE, THE WORK OF GIUSEPPE VALAPERTA, A GIFTED SCULPTOR MUCH ADMIRED BY LATROBE. THIS PARTICULAR EAGLE—HIS ONLY PIECE IN THE CAPITOL—WAS NOT AMONG HIS BEST WORKS AND THE RIDICULE IT AROUSED IS BELIEVED TO HAVE DRIVEN HIM TO SUICIDE. *FACING PAGE:* IN STATUARY HALL, THE *CAR OF HISTORY*, BY CARLO FRANZONI, SHOWS CLIO, THE MUSE OF HISTORY, IN A WINGED CHARIOT, RECORDING THE EVENTS UNFOLDING BEFORE HER. IN THE WHEEL OF THE CHARIOT IS A CLOCK, MADE BY AMERICAN CLOCKMAKER SIMON WILLARD, WHICH FOR MANY YEARS WAS THE OFFICIAL TIMEKEEPER OF THE HOUSE. THE CHARIOT PASSES OVER THE GLOBE, ON WHICH ARE CARVED THE SIGNS OF THE ZODIAC. CARLO FRANZONI WAS BROUGHT TO WASHINGTON FROM ITALY AFTER THE DEATH OF HIS BROTHER GIUSEPPE, WHO HAD CARVED THE MUCH-ADMIRED "CORNCOB CAPITALS." CARLO FRANZONI IS SAID TO HAVE USED ONE OF HIS BROTHER'S DAUGHTERS AS HIS MODEL FOR CLIO.

came to Washington at Jefferson's behest to decorate the Capitol. Above the north entrance to the Hall is the marble *Car of History* by Carlo Franzoni, in which Clio, the Muse of History, in shown standing in a winged chariot. In a niche over the south entrance stands *Liberty and the Eagle* by Enrico Causici.

A famous painting of the House in session in 1822 by Samuel F. B. Morse proved invaluable as a guide to restoring Statuary Hall as nearly as possible to the way it looked when used by the House of Representatives. The painting, now in the Corcoran Gallery of Art, enabled faithful reproductions of the chandelier, sconces, and draperies to be made, and the elegance, if not the function, of the original room has been masterfully recalled. Beautiful, but never too successful as a legislative chamber, the old Hall of the House has had a felicitous rebirth as National Statuary Hall.

OFFICES

OF

PRIVILEGE

THE ANNOUNCEMENT of the competition to design the Capitol in 1792 made no mention of office space for congressmen, and this was not an oversight. Congressional service then, and well into the nineteenth century, was very different from what it would become in the latter part of the twentieth. Sessions were generally shorter; rarely was a Member required to spend even as much as half of his time in Washington. Nor did many expect to make a career of the job; turnover was high. Service in Washington was seen as a valuable addition to one's record—something worth devoting a few years to before returning to the much more dynamic and

powerful arena of local politics. Members had no staff, and any visiting constituents were received on the House or Senate floor. For that, Members' desks were adequate office space.

~ During the nineteenth century, however, as the nation and its commerce and concerns grew, so did the business of Congress. Constituencies were becoming larger, and improved transportation systems were delivering an ever-increasing number of those constituents to the Capitol to look in on their representatives. Congressional service became more professional, with Members more inclined to seek multiple terms and to take a longer view of what they required to

FACING PAGE: THE PRESIDENT'S
ROOM, IN THE SENATE WING.
ABOVE: BRONZE FIGURES FROM
THE PRESIDENT'S ROOM CHAN-
DELIER, IN FRONT OF
LIBERTY, ONE OF BRUMIDI'S
MADONNA-LIKE FIGURES.

be effective while in office. One pressing need stood out, and in the 1880s Congress authorized each Member to hire a staff of one. After that, any illusions that all the business of government could be conducted within the Capitol were quickly dispelled. In 1908, the Cannon House Office Building was opened southeast of the Capitol; a mirror image of it, the Russell Senate Office Building, was opened the following year to the northeast. For the first time in the history of Congress, each Member had an office.

If Thornton gave short shrift to offices in his design, the more practical Latrobe built numerous committee rooms and storage areas on the ground floor of the House wing; Bulfinch added still more, and Walter made what seemed at the time to be more than adequate provision for them in the Senate and House extensions in the 1850s. But those offices were never intended for the rank and file; they were to accommodate the constitutional and other elected officers of Congress.

There are only two constitutionally mandated congressional officers: a Presiding Officer for each chamber. Beyond that, Congress was left to invent itself. In the House of Representatives the Presiding Officer is the Speaker, elected by the Members at the start of each Congress. The vice president presides over the Senate; however, in his absence the Senate elects a President pro tempore—traditionally the senior Member of the majority party. The roles of the two Presiding Officers have developed in dramatically different ways. The office of President pro tempore of the Senate is a largely ceremonial one, while the Speaker of the House wields enormous political power, largely the legacy of the individuals who have held the position and established the necessary precedents.

The elected officers of Congress are those responsible for its day-to-day management. Some positions are as old as Congress itself, although

THE WORKING OFFICE OF THE
SPEAKER OF THE HOUSE, IN A
PART OF THE CAPITOL CREATED
WHEN THE EAST FRONT WAS
EXTENDED. *FACING PAGE:* THE
SPEAKER ALSO HAS A CERE-
MONIAL OFFICE, A ROOM THAT
SHOWS THE TASTEFUL SKILL OF
THOMAS U. WALTER. THE ROOM
HOUSED VARIOUS COMMITTEES
BEFORE BEING ASSIGNED TO
THE SPEAKER OF THE HOUSE
IN 1908. THE CHANDELIER USED
TO HANG IN THE WHITE HOUSE
AND WAS BOUGHT AT AUCTION
WHEN THE WHITE HOUSE WAS
BEING REBUILT IN 1902. THE
CARPET HAS BEEN CUT TO
REVEAL A SECTION OF THE
ORIGINAL MINTON TILE.

aspects of the jobs today would be unrecognizable to the earlier incum-
bents. Officers are elected by the membership of each house, which is to
say by the majority party of each house, at the beginning of every Congress. The chief administrative officers are the Secretary of the Senate
and the Clerk of the House. Both houses elect a Sergeant at Arms to
enforce the rules of Congress and, if necessary, round up stray Members
for a vote. The House elects a Doorkeeper, who, among his other administrative duties, announces official visitors at the door and enforces
the rules of the chamber. All of these officials have offices in the Capitol.

Each house also has a parliamentarian who needs an office near to
the chamber; either he or an assistant must always be present during
sessions to ensure that proper parliamentary procedures are followed.
Parliamentarians are chosen by the majority leadership, with whom
they work closely, but they must also provide impartial information to
both parties. They need to be well versed in precedents and the work-
ings of their respective chambers in order to give advice on the most
effective way to get things done.

The political hierarchy that exists in Congress today is the result of
an evolutionary process. There were no political parties when the

Constitution was written, and the factions that did exist were decried by many, including George Washington. In his Farewell Address he warned "in the most solemn manner against the baneful effects of the spirit of party generally." Parties, in his view, tended to misrepresent the opinions of others in order to acquire influence, and thus "render alien to each other those who ought to be bound together by fraternal affection." Despite his warning, over the years a two-party system did develop, and by the 1820s was already well established in Congressional elections.

The party leaders of both houses have offices in the Capitol. Each house has a majority and a minority leader, and a majority and minority whip, elected at the beginning of each Congress.

The majority leaders are able to expedite or impede legislation, a power they exercise in getting their party's program enacted. Minority leaders are more limited in what they can do, although—particularly in the Senate—an irritated minority leader can be troublesome.

The term "whip," long in use in the British Parliament, comes from the men whose job during a fox hunt is to "whip in" the hounds and make sure they keep their focus on the business at hand—in that case, the fox. It is an apt comparison with the duties of the whips; they try to keep the attention of party members focused on the leadership's program. And especially in the House, with its larger number of Members, whips try to keep the leadership aware of the Members' sentiments. Sometimes a whip helps the undecided by standing at the door to the chamber, with thumb up or down, indicating how they should vote.

Generally speaking, the offices assigned are commensurate with the prestige of the occupant. The Speaker of the House, in addition to his working offices and private dining room, has a ceremonial office in the House extension, where he holds press conferences before the opening of each session and greets visiting dignitaries. On the Senate side, the Republican leader occupies a suite of rooms—now known as the Howard H. Baker, Jr., Rooms—in one of the oldest parts of the Capitol.

The Senate Democratic leader occupies the Robert C. Byrd Rooms in the extension. His office holds a record: as the office of the Secretary of the Senate from 1859 until the mid-1980s, it was used continually for the same purpose longer than any other room in the building.

Indeed, possibly the most striking feature of the room assignments in the Capitol is their impermanence. Records from the early years are sketchy, but even picking up the story in the middle, we find that most of the rooms have served many different purposes—the result of practical considerations and the privileges of seniority. Nowhere does

seniority weigh more heavily than in the allocation of the so-called "hideaway" offices of certain senior senators.

Once a perquisite enjoyed by only the most senior among them, now most senators are allotted one of these very private, very coveted sanctums. So intensely is their privacy guarded that the rooms are not listed in the Congressional Directory. They are tucked away on all the floors on the Senate side of the Capitol, from the basement to the attic. Most would be impossible to find without a guide, but then again, the need would never arise. Some belonging to senior senators are spacious and even elegant, while a junior senator may have to bide time in a windowless closet before qualifying for something a little better; room assignment is based strictly on seniority.

Some offices are above periodic reshuffling. Among them are those that Walter provided for the President and vice president in the extensions. In conjunction with his role as president of the Senate, the vice president maintains a staff and has a ceremonial office in the Capitol. It was in the ceremonial office that vice president Henry Wilson died after suffering a stroke in 1875. There is a bust of him there, and under it a plaque describing the revered former senator as a man who began as a journeyman shoemaker, lived and died poor, and yet "left to his grateful countrymen the memory of an honorable public service, and a good name far better than riches."

FACING PAGE: THE SENATE REPUBLICAN LEADER'S OFFICE IN THE HOWARD H. BAKER, JR., ROOMS. DIRECTLY ACROSS FROM THE OLD SENATE CHAMBER, THE ROOM HAS HAD A UTILI- TARIAN PAST: IT FIRST HOUSED

The President's Room originally was designed to be an office for the President, but its name has become something of a misnomer: the President hardly ever goes there anymore. The competition of 1792 made no mention of a room for the President, and although a room so designated appears in one of Latrobe's drawings, there is no evidence that such a room ever existed until the extensions were added. Before the passage of the Twentieth Amendment in 1933, the President's term ended on March 4, the last day of Congress. The President used to come to this room to sign last-minute bills and appointments before his term expired. After 1933 the room was no longer needed for that purpose, but it is occasionally used for symbolic reasons. On August 6, 1965, in what he called the keeping of a promise, Lyndon Johnson signed the Voting Rights Act of 1965 there—104 years to the day after Abraham Lincoln had in the same room signed a bill freeing slaves who had been pressed into service under the Confederacy.

THE SECRETARY OF THE SENATE, AND—WHEN THE SUPREME COURT TOOK OVER THE CHAM- BER—CLERKS OF THE COURT. IT IS ONE OF THE LARGEST ROOMS IN THE ORIGINAL SENATE WING. *ABOVE:* THE MANTELPIECE WITH A BUST OF PRESIDENT DWIGHT D. EISENHOWER.

What the President's Room lacks in purpose, it makes up in splendor. The frescoes on the ceilings and the oil paintings on the walls show Constantino Brumidi's art at its apogee. Brumidi wove together portraits

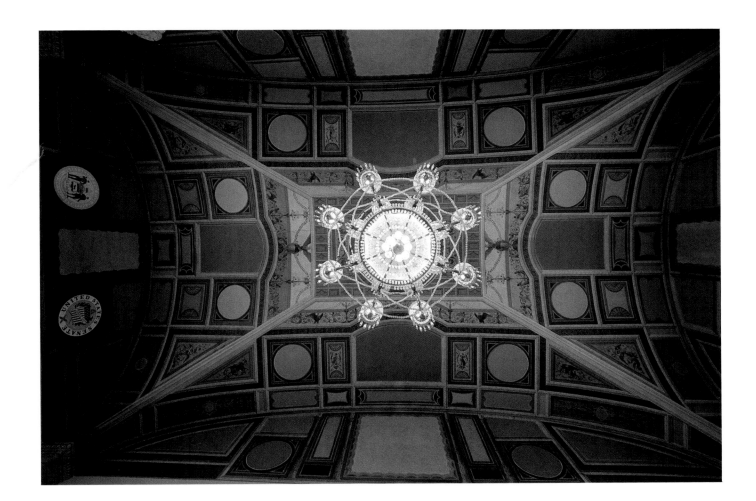

and allegory to illustrate the role of the chief executive. In medallions on the walls are the five members of George Washington's first Cabinet: Thomas Jefferson, Alexander Hamilton, Henry Knox, Samuel Osgood, and Edmund Randolph. In the four corners, next to the ceiling, are full-length portraits representing Religion (William Brewster), Discovery (Christopher Columbus), History (Benjamin Franklin), and Exploration (Amerigo Vespucci). Madonna-like figures in the ceiling symbolize four tenets upon which the country's government is built: Liberty, Legislation, Executive Authority, and Religion. Of course, George Washington is also there. Brumidi copied in fresco the "porthole" portrait by Rembrandt Peale that now hangs in the Old Senate Chamber, placing a figure of Victory on one side, and Peace on the other. Lavishly interspersed are Brumidi's trademark cherubs and floral garlands.

Because the room was carpeted for many years, the Minton tiles on the floor have retained their original vibrancy. The chandelier that dominates the room is one of the few original—and certainly one of the largest—chandeliers in the Capitol. Hung in 1864, it was one of hundreds of gas fixtures made by the Philadelphia firm of Cornelius and Baker. They would have been collectors' items today, but after a serious gas explosion in the Capitol in 1898 heightened the ever-present fear of fire, most of them went on the auction block. The chandelier in the

FACING PAGE: THE JOHN F. KENNEDY ROOM, SO CALLED BECAUSE THE DEMOCRATIC LEADERSHIP GAVE IT TO HIM TO USE BETWEEN HIS ELECTION AND INAUGURATION. (AS A JUNIOR SENATOR, HE DID NOT OTHERWISE RATE A ROOM IN THE CAPITOL.) SINCE 1987 IT HAS BEEN THE SECRETARY OF THE SENATE'S OFFICE. *TOP AND BOTTOM:* THE CEILING, AND A PUTTI-AND-SHIELD DETAIL.

A SENATORIAL "HIDEAWAY"
ON THE THIRD FLOOR IN THE
OLDEST PART OF THE BUILD-
ING; ITS WALLS STILL CONCEAL
CHARRED TIMBERS FROM THE
FIRE OF 1814. LATROBE'S ORIGI-
NAL PURPOSE FOR THE ROOM
IS UNCERTAIN, BUT ITS SOME-
WHAT INCONVENIENT LOCA-
TION DOOMED IT TO SERVICE
AS A UTILITY AREA. ONLY IN
1983, WHEN THE CLUTTER WAS
CLEARED AWAY, WERE THE POS-
SIBILITIES OF THIS HANDSOME
VAULTED SPACE RECOGNIZED,
AND IT WAS QUICKLY CLAIMED
AS A PRIVATE OFFICE. *FACING
PAGE:* ONE OF THE MORE SPA-
CIOUS "HIDEAWAY" OFFICES,
OFF THE BRUMIDI CORRIDOR.

President's Room was spared, electrified, and, in what has been described as an act of supererogation, enlarged; in 1915 six additional branches were added to the eighteen original ones. The President's Room, with its paintings and decorations, tiles and original furnishings, is virtually un-changed since the late nineteenth century. Many consider it the finest room in the Capitol.

Facing page: The Vice President's ceremonial office. The chandelier once hung in the White House. The desk has been used by every vice president since the late nineteenth century, except for a brief stint when President Nixon took it with him to the White House (and injudiciously kept activating devices for recording machines in its drawers). *Top:* The clock has been in the vice president's office since 1887. *Bottom:* Detail of the ornate gilt mirror, part of the room's original furnishings.

CONGRESS
AT
WORK

T HE FIRST CONGRESS convened
in 1789, and while waiting for
President-elect George Washington to arrive, the House and Senate
set about the task of electing their first
officers and adopting their separate
rules of procedure. One of the first
matters to be decided concerned committees, which experience from colonial legislatures and the Continental
Congress had shown to be the most
efficient way to conduct business
within a larger legislative body.
⌒ Most of the early
committees were ad hoc
—created to deal with
single legislative issues
as they arose. It was not
long, however, before
the House and Senate
developed a perma-

nent, or standing, committee system.
The House Committee on Ways and
Means, which originated as an ad hoc
committee in 1789, became permanent
in 1802. The precursor of the House
Committee on Commerce and Man-
ufactures became a standing committee as early as 1795. In 1816 the Senate
appointed its first standing committees, heralding a seminal change in
the way Congress would work. Standing committees carried over from one
Congress to the next; they developed
the necessary expertise
to deal with complex
issues and began to take
a more active, rather
than reactive, role in
setting the congres-
sional agenda. ⌒ In
the early, crowded years

A CLASSICAL MAIDEN BY
BRUMIDI IN THE SENATE
APPROPRIATIONS COMMITTEE
ROOM, FORMERLY THE NAVAL
AFFAIRS COMMITTEE ROOM.
FACING PAGE: THE ORNATELY
DECORATED SENATE RECEP-
TION ROOM.

of the Capitol, committees met wherever they could find space—even in corners of the Senate Chamber. Both Latrobe and Bulfinch, however, provided a number of meeting rooms in their later plans, and in designing the Capitol extensions, Thomas U. Walter made ample provision for the ever-increasing number of committees. By 1860 each committee had a room and one clerk, or, it could more accurately be said, each committee *chairman* had an office and a secretary. Those were enviable bonuses, and a chairmanship—any chairmanship—was worth having. Not surprisingly, it proved easier to form new committees than to disband existing ones. Some committees rattled along for years, neither meeting nor reporting out legislation, but providing office space and a clerk for their fortunate chairmen. The Senate Committee on Revolutionary War Claims, for example, continued to exist long after any veterans from that war, or their survivors, were in need of temporal advocates.

Committees also grew in power; in 1885 future President Woodrow Wilson lamented that what the country had was "a government by the chairmen of the Standing Committees of Congress." However, the opening of the first House and Senate office buildings in 1908 and 1909 provided each Member with an office, and that effectively eliminated the value of a meaningless committee chairmanship. The way was cleared for reform of the system; the number of standing committees was sharply reduced in 1920, and more than halved in 1946 by the Legislative Reorganization Act. Nevertheless, in both houses committee work still represents the greater part of a Member's responsibilities, and it is generally through work on committees that congressional reputations are made. As Woodrow Wilson also said, "Congress in session is Congress on public exhibition, whilst Congress in committee-rooms is Congress at work."

Few committees meet in the Capitol today; most have moved to more commodious quarters in one of the House or Senate office buildings. Exceptions are the Appropriations Committees of both houses, certainly the largest and among the most influential of all the committees. The Senate Foreign Relations Committee continues to meet in the Capitol; that august building is considered a more appropriate place in which to receive foreign dignitaries.

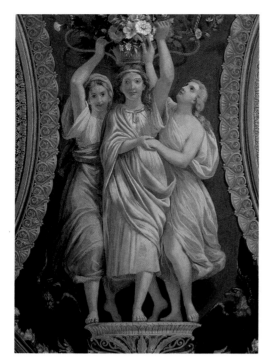

It was in a committee room that Constantino Brumidi was first given the opportunity to demonstrate the art of fresco. At his request, and at his own expense, Captain Meigs allowed him to paint a lunette in the room that was to be assigned to the House Committee on Agriculture. Since Brumidi was Italian, Meigs suggested as a topic Cincinnatus, a Roman hero of the fifth century B.C., who left his farm to rush to the defense of Rome. George Washington, also a farmer, was often compared with Cincinnatus. Brumidi's fresco, *The Calling of Cincinnatus from the Plow,* was an immediate success. (Only when they had seen more of it would Brumidi's detractors begin to complain that his art was too "European.") A relieved Meigs reported that "even strict economists and men from the western wilderness expressed their satisfaction and encouraged [him] to go on." Go on Brumidi did, balancing the lunette of Cincinnatus with a parallel story from the American Revolution, *The Calling of Putnam from the Plow to the Revolution.* (Israel Putnam left his farm to command the defense in the Battle of Breed's Hill, more commonly known as the Battle of Bunker Hill.) Two small panels on opposite walls contrast a primitive method of cutting grain—with a sickle—with what was then the state-of-the-art invention, the McCormick Reaper. On the ceiling Brumidi painted charming allegorical groupings representing the four seasons. The room is now occupied by a subcommittee of the House Appropriations Committee.

The Senate Appropriations Committee also has rooms that were decorated for earlier tenants: the committees on Military Affairs and on Naval Affairs. In the former, Brumidi painted five large battle scenes from American Revolutionary history; an able English artist, James Leslie, painted wall panels filled with military paraphernalia. The decorations of the Naval Affairs Committee room are among Brumidi's finest. In the vaults of the ceiling are mythological figures relating to the seas, and in each of nine large wall panels is a charming water nymph.

Not all of the work of Congress takes place in committee rooms and offices. Each house has a reception room, conveniently located near the chamber, where members meet with constituents or lobbyists. The House has the Sam

AMERICA

THE SAM RAYBURN ROOM, THE RECEPTION ROOM OF THE HOUSE OF REPRESENTATIVES, WAS BUILT DURING THE EXTENSION OF THE EAST FRONT IN 1962. REPRODUCTIONS OF EIGHTEENTH- AND NINETEENTH-CENTURY FURNISHINGS INCLUDE CHIPPENDALE CHAIRS, DUNCAN PHYFE SOFAS, AND HEPPLEWHITE TABLES. THE HUGE SÈVRES VASES WERE A GIFT FROM FRANCE, IN "SISTERLY GRATITUDE FOR AMERICA'S TIMELY HELP" IN WORLD WAR I; THE SENATE ALSO HAS A PAIR. *PAGE 150:* PART OF BRUMIDI'S CEILING DECORATION REFLECTED IN A MIRROR OF THE SENATE RECEPTION ROOM. THE LAVISH ICONOGRAPHY OF THE ROOM INCLUDES RATTLESNAKES, CONSIDERED AN APT SYMBOL OF THE UNITED STATES BECAUSE THEY NEVER STRIKE WITHOUT WARNING, AND NEVER STRIKE UNLESS PROVOKED. *PAGE 151:* THE "GREAT TRIUMVIRATE" OF THE NINETEENTH-CENTURY SENATE WAS AN OBVIOUS CHOICE TO FILL THREE OF THE FIVE "PORTHOLES" LEFT EMPTY BY BRUMIDI IN THE SENATE RECEPTION ROOM. *TOP TO BOTTOM:* JOHN C. CALHOUN, HENRY CLAY, AND DANIEL WEBSTER.

Rayburn Room, located in the East Front extension and dedicated in 1962 to the memory of the longest-serving Speaker of the House. (Sam Rayburn and his fellow Texan Lyndon Johnson were such driving forces behind the East Front extension that preservationists who opposed the project—and they were many—referred to it as the "Texas Front.") The quietly refined room, with walnut paneling and columns, is a good example of the Colonial Revival style. On the other side of the building, the Senate Reception Room stands in complete contrast; here are decoration and ornamentation taken to the limit. Completed when the extensions were added in the mid-nineteenth century, this was a room visiting foreigners might see, a room that would say something about the aesthetic and economic state of the young country. No expense was spared in making it impressive. The ornamental plasterwork is by Ernest Thomas, a French craftsman. He was urged by Meigs to be sure to make a "good show" of it, since some of the men working for him were complaining about being under the supervision of a "foreigner" and needed some positive reinforcement. Thomas *did* make a good show of it; the room has every possible plaster embellishment. Brumidi then added his artistic contribution; on one half of the ceiling are groups representing Peace, Freedom, War, and Plenty, and on the other half are the four cardinal virtues, Prudence, Justice, Temperance, and Fortitude. On the south wall is a fresco of Washington in consultation with Jefferson and Hamilton. Brumidi left five "portholes" empty. Nearly a century later it was decided to fill them with portraits of people who had made outstanding contributions to the Senate, and a freshman senator from Massachusetts was put in charge of a special committee to determine who they should be. John F. Kennedy, chosen on the strength of his book *Profiles in Courage,* described it as "nearly an impossible task," but in 1959 the five choices were unveiled: Daniel Webster, John C. Calhoun, and Henry Clay, the preeminent senators of the nineteenth century, together with conservative Robert A. Taft and liberal Robert M. La Follette, Sr., of the twentieth.

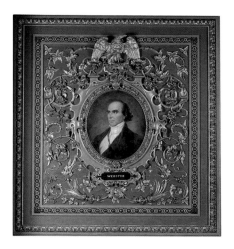

Members of Congress have several sanctuaries to which they can retreat and be among their colleagues. One is the so-called Board of Education Room, where education of a distinctly nontraditional kind takes place. The room originally was occupied by the Committee on Territories, but since 1901 the room has come under the control of the Speakers of the House. Two of them, Nicholas Longworth and John Nance Garner, often invited congressional colleagues to join them there because, as Garner said, "You get a couple of drinks in a young Congressman and then you know what he knows and what he can do." Sam Rayburn carried on the practice with his legendary bourbon and branch water. In an era when many Members did not bring their families to Washington, "Rayburn's lieutenants" and cronies from both houses regularly gathered there at the end of the day. Vice president Harry S. Truman was with Rayburn, talking, as he put it, "Of shoes—and ships—and sealing-wax—Of cabbages—and kings," when he received an urgent summons to the White House. He raced back to his office to collect his hat and presented himself at the White House, there to learn that Franklin Roosevelt had died and that he was now President.

There is another sanctuary to which most members of Congress need a special invitation: the Lindy Claiborne Boggs Congressional Women's Reading Room. Congresswomen use the room for reading, relaxing, and holding meetings; congressmen enter only when invited, or, if they wish to schedule a meeting there, by making arrangements through one of the congresswomen. History was made in 1916 when Jeannette Rankin of Montana became the first woman elected to Congress. Six years later the first woman senator was sworn in, appointed to fill an unexpired term. By a bizarre set of circumstances the eighty-seven-year-old Rebecca Latimer Felton of Georgia held her Senate seat for only one day, but she seized the opportunity that day to promise her fellow senators: "When the women of the country come in and sit with you, though there may be but a very few in the next few years, I pledge you that you will get ability, you will get integrity of purpose, you will get exalted patriotism and you will get unstinted usefulness." By the middle of the twentieth century there were enough congresswomen to warrant a room of their own, and in 1962 they were given one just off Statuary Hall, designed by Latrobe and imbued with history. It was renamed in 1990 in honor of Lindy Boggs's long association with Congress and distinguished record of public service.

FACING PAGE: THE LINDY CLAIBORNE BOGGS CONGRESSIONAL WOMEN'S READING ROOM, IN WHAT IS THOUGHT TO BE ONE OF THE FEW ROOMS IN THE CAPITOL TO HAVE SURVIVED THE FIRE OF 1814. CONVENIENTLY LOCATED NEXT TO WHAT WAS THEN THE HALL OF THE HOUSE, IT WAS THE SPEAKER'S OFFICE BEFORE THE EXTENSIONS WERE ADDED; ONE OF ITS FIRST OCCUPANTS WAS HENRY CLAY. TO THIS ROOM JOHN QUINCY ADAMS WAS CARRIED IN 1848 AFTER COLLAPSING IN THE HALL OF THE HOUSE, AND HERE, TWO DAYS LATER, HE DIED. HIS BUST IS DISPLAYED AGAINST THE WALL.

ART

AND THE

CAPITOL

THE DISCREET RELATIONSHIP between art and politics posed a dilemma for the young republic. On the one hand, Americans were intent on establishing their own identity and cutting the ties with what they considered the decadent societies of Europe. This depended first and foremost on economic viability, and many believed all exertions should be directed toward this end. Benjamin Franklin thought the refinements of art proper for an older country, but for America ". . . the invention of a machine or the improvement of an implement is of more importance than a masterpiece of Raphael." John Adams concurred, writing to his wife, Abigail: "I must study politics and war, that my sons may have liberty to study mathematics and philosophy, geography, natural history and naval architecture, navigation, commerce, and agriculture, in order to give their children a right to study painting, poetry, music, architecture, statuary, tapestry, and porcelain." Art was a luxury. At the same time some Americans bristled at any suggestion of materialism, and were embarrassed at what they perceived as their cultural inferiority. Those who had been influenced by the Enlightenment recognized the importance of encouraging the cultural life of the new republic. But what kind of culture? Nationalists

BRONZE BUST OF GEORGE WASHINGTON BY P. J. DAVID D'ANGERS IN THE ROTUNDA. *FACING PAGE:* BRUMIDI'S *THE FOUR SEASONS*, ON THE CEILING OF THE ROOM ORIGINALLY OCCUPIED BY THE HOUSE COMMITTEE ON AGRICULTURE.

argued that America must develop its own artistic voice; others remained loyal to the ideals of neoclassicism then coming into vogue throughout Europe.

Furthermore, there was the matter of money. There simply was not yet sufficient private wealth to provide the level of patronage common among the royal houses of Europe. Nor was Congress eager to assume the role of patron of the arts. With so many other pressing claims on the public purse, spending money on "luxuries" was a sure way to make enemies. Still, was not artistic talent something that ought to be supported by a democratic government? Had not Athens done as much?

There was yet another stumbling block during the early decades of the Capitol. Despite an understandable desire to have American artists work on the building, there were few of them, and fewer still qualified to undertake the kind of work needed: neoclassical sculpture and large, historical paintings. People like Latrobe and Meigs understood that skill mattered more than national origin, but not all congressmen did.

Such conflicting views led to a somewhat haphazard approach to commissioning works of art for the Capitol, and the result is a diverse collection of painting and sculpture, parts of which can compete with holdings of the greatest museums in the world and parts of which are mediocre at best. Perhaps this too is a fitting reflection of the variety and differences found among the owners of the collection. No officially sanctioned arbiter of taste ruled here. It is doubtless safe to say that there is not one work of art in the Capitol that someone, somewhere, does not find inspiring.

There are several collections of sculpture in the Capitol. The largest, of course, is the National Statuary Hall Collection. Presidents, with the exception of Washington, Jefferson, and Lincoln, are not well represented since they have no official role in Congress. Vice presidents fare much better because they also serve as president of the Senate. In 1875 the well-loved vice president Henry Wilson died in the Capitol after suffering a stroke, and a bust by sculptor Augustus Saint-Gaudens was commissioned in his memory. Thereafter it was decided to honor every vice president in a similar way. Wilson's bust is in the ceremonial office of the vice president, and the busts of the twenty other earliest vice presidents are located appropriately in niches around the Senate Chamber. Later ones are found in nearby corridors.

The first government commission for paintings went to John Trumbull in 1817, to produce "four paintings, commemorative of the most important events in the American Revolution" for four of the eight panels around the wall of the Rotunda. As would be the case time and

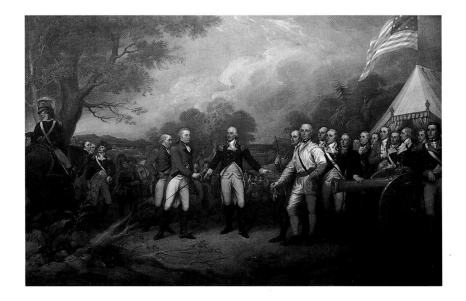

again, however, the finished work met with congressional disapproval. As unschooled as they might be in matters of aesthetics, Members knew what they did *not* like, and they could be counted on to muster their highest gifts of scorn and oratory in denouncing what they saw. Trumbull's works, now considered to be among the most important paintings in the Capitol, were dismissed as "solemn daubing," and the unenthusiastic reception accorded them, together with the tightfisted attitude of Congress, appears to have stifled at the time any movement to complete the four remaining panels in the Rotunda. Commissions eventually were awarded to four different artists in 1836; their work met with no more congressional approval than Trumbull's had.

The proposed extension to the Capitol meant new walls to be covered, and promised a spate of government commissions for works of art with which to cover them. Petitions began pouring in from artists eager to be considered. Most of the works commissioned during the 1850s bore Meigs's stamp of approval, and undoubtedly his greatest contribution to the Capitol was his selection and unwavering support of Constantino Brumidi.

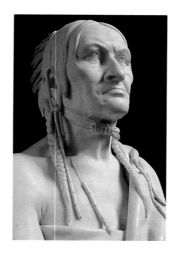

Top: A BUST OF BEESHEKEE, OR BUFFALO, A LEADER OF THE CHIPPEWA TRIBE, STANDS IN A SENATE CORRIDOR. THE CHIEF VISITED WASHINGTON AS PART OF A NATIVE AMERICAN DELEGATION TO DISCUSS TREATIES WITH THE GOVERNMENT, AND WHILE HERE, MEIGS ASKED HIM TO SIT FOR A BUST BY FRANCIS VINCENTI, A SCULPTOR THEN WORKING ON THE EXTENSIONS. MEIGS THOUGHT IT WOULD BE AN INTERESTING RECORD OF THE INDIAN CULTURE "FIVE HUNDRED YEARS HENCE." SO WELL DID IT TURN OUT THAT A SIMILAR BUST WAS LATER DONE IN BRONZE FOR THE HOUSE. BEESHEKEE, HOWEVER, DIED SOON AFTER; SOME MAINTAINED THAT THE MODEL HAD DRAINED THE LIFE FROM HIM. *Bottom:* A BRONZE ENTITLED *INDIAN FOUNTAIN* BY WILLIAM H. RINEHART, IN THE OFFICE OF THE ARCHITECT OF THE CAPITOL.

Brumidi was born in Rome in 1805 and studied at the Accademia di San Luca with Antonio Canova. A captain in the National Guard, he was imprisoned during an uprising, given a papal pardon, and advised to leave Italy; in 1852 he arrived in New York. He had become expert in the art of fresco after being commissioned by the pope to restore the frescoes of one loggia in the Vatican. Fresco painting, in which the pigment is applied directly to the still-wet plaster, is a highly demanding and unforgiving art. Brumidi thought only fresco worthy of the Capitol, and Meigs, too, considered it to be "the highest style of architectural decoration." Brumidi asked Meigs to allow him a section of wall on which to demonstrate his talents—it being impractical for him to carry samples of his work around with him—and in 1855 he began the work that would occupy him until his death in 1880.

Brumidi's style, at first acclaimed, was soon encountering criticism for its heavy emphasis on classical motifs. Representative Owen Lovejoy said of the earliest frescoes: "Overhead we have pictures of Bacchus, Ceres, and so on surrounded with cupids, cherubs, etc. to the end of heathen mythology. All this we have, but not a single specimen of the valuable breeds of cattle, horses, sheep, etc., which are now found in the country." The consensus was that his work was too European; his supporters, who were few but influential, maintained that American taste was not sufficiently developed to appreciate Brumidi.

In 1857, when the commission for a large battle scene for one of the staircases in the extension was awarded to a Frenchman, Horace Vernet, matters came to a head. A group of American artists, led by Rembrandt Peale, petitioned Congress to protest the employment of foreign artists and to urge Congress to encourage the development of a national art by awarding commissions to Americans. If there were no Americans capable of doing what was required, they continued, "a plain coat of whitewash" on the walls would be preferable to giving the work to foreigners. The artists requested that an art commission be appointed to approve the funds being spent for art. Congress, having little faith in what they had seen of Meigs's taste or Brumidi's work, readily agreed.

The Art Commission issued one report, criticizing Brumidi for "painting rooms in the style of the loggias of Raphael, the baths of Titus and Pompeii," and disapproving of the "gaudy" and "inharmonious" colors he was using in the corridors of the new Senate wing—colors that would make "calm thought and unimpassioned reason" quite impossible. In its defense, the mandate given the Commission had been vague. But its accomplishments were few. It was disbanded the following year. Thereafter the Joint Committee on the Library of Congress continued to commission and buy works—more and more by American artists.

The criteria for acquiring works of art for the Capitol have never been those of artistic merit alone. Some pieces, such as Trumbull's paintings in the Rotunda, are valuable as historical records. *The First Reading of the Emancipation Proclamation,* by Francis Bicknell Carpenter, was actually painted in the East Room of the White House and includes fine individual portraits of Lincoln's Cabinet. Brigadier General Seth Eastman was commissioned to paint, from firsthand experience, seventeen pictures of historic forts and nine of Indian scenes; they are invaluable documents today. Yet despite the lack of a well-articulated policy on the acquisition of works of art, and the political pressures ever attendant on those responsible for commissioning and purchasing work, the collection contains a number of masterpieces. Represented on the Capitol walls are Charles Willson Peale and his celebrated son, Rembrandt; Gilbert Stuart; John Trumbull; Thomas Sully; Eastman

Johnson; Albert Bierstadt; and John Singer Sargent. Within the Capitol walls are the works of sculptors such as Hiram Powers, Thomas Crawford, Augustus Saint-Gaudens, and Daniel Chester French.

More than anything else, perhaps, the paintings and sculptures in the Capitol are important for what they reveal about those who assembled the collection. In it can be seen the people Americans admire, the achievements of which they are proud, and the religious and political principles they hold dear.

THE HOUSE:
HERE, SIR,
THE PEOPLE GOVERN

On December 16, 1857, Members of the House of Representatives held the first session in their new chamber. It was then—and still is—one of the largest legislative chambers in the world, easily able to accommodate an oak desk and chair for each of the 237 Members. More than a thousand spectators could sit in the galleries that ran around four sides of the room. The coffered cast-iron ceiling had skylights with the seal of a state or territory in the center of most. Fifteen hundred "newfangled" gas jets above the glass provided a soft light at night. Most important of all, the chamber offered the Members what they had lacked heretofore: a room in which they could hear and be heard. ∾ There were drawbacks, of course. Ventilation was poor; Meigs's relocation of the chamber to the center of the wing allowed it to be surrounded by committee rooms and offices, but not by what Members were used to: windows that could be opened to admit fresh air. Nor did the elaborate system of air ducts fully appease them; Senator John P. Hale stoutly rebuked the builders for presuming that they could come up with a better arrangement for supplying light and air than the Almighty had done. The room was sometimes dark, and when it rained the noise on the skylights was disruptive. Most of the problems of

Facing page: THREE ROOMS WERE COMBINED TO CREATE THE REPRESENTATIVES' RETIRING ROOMS; THE MIDDLE ROOM WAS FORMERLY THE SPEAKER'S OFFICE. THE PINEAPPLE MOTIF IN THE CEILING, *ABOVE*, IS A SYMBOL OF HOSPITALITY.

the chamber, however, were solved by the march of progress. By the end of the nineteenth century electric lighting was replacing gas, and in the late 1920s air conditioning was added. Moreover, Congress made sure it would not outgrow the chamber by passing a law in 1911 limiting the number of representatives to 435, the distribution of seats to be adjusted by the census taken every ten years, with each state getting at least one.

The House of Representatives met in its chamber for nearly a century before major changes became necessary. A 1938 survey showed the cast-iron-and-glass roofing of the House and Senate chambers to be in danger of collapsing, and the repairs that were authorized ended up being a complete remodeling of both chambers. The work was delayed by World War II, but on January 1, 1951, the House moved back into what was essentially a new chamber in its old space.

The need for remodeling the room was unassailable. The ceilings were replaced with stainless steel structural beams, trusses, and reinforced-concrete slabs; Members could again assemble without fear of the roof falling in on them. Lighting and air-conditioning systems were upgraded, and a public-address system permitted the loudspeakers, which formerly had hung from the ceiling, to be concealed.

The aesthetic aim of the architects was to replicate, or at least suggest, early Federal architecture. All remnants of Victorian taste were eliminated in favor of a somewhat plain, but functional, room. And, in an era when little thought was given to preservation, the sole reminders of the old room are the portraits of Lafayette and Washington on either side of the Speaker's rostrum, the mace, and an inkwell on the Speaker's desk.

Apart from the two portraits, the only representational art in the chamber are relief portraits on the gallery wall of twenty-three lawgivers—men who have played some part in the evolution of the laws of civilization—from Hammurabi to Napoleon. Two Americans, George Mason and Thomas Jefferson, are among them. Moses takes center stage, directly opposite the Speaker's chair. All others are shown in profile, eleven facing right and eleven facing left. A plaque above the Speaker's chair bears a quotation from Daniel Webster:

> Let us develop the resources of our land, call forth its powers, build up its institutions, promote all its great interests and see whether we also in our day and generation may not perform something worthy to be remembered.

The House of Representatives has historically been the body most

THE CHERUBIC BRONZE WALL SCONCES IN THE REPRESENTATIVES' RETIRING ROOMS ORIGINALLY WERE GAS-FUELED AND ARE AMONG THE OLDEST LIGHT FIXTURES STILL IN USE IN THE CAPITOL. *FACING PAGE:* THE EAST DOORS INTO THE HOUSE CHAMBER. *PAGES 164-65:* ON THE WALLS OF THE SPEAKER'S LOBBY, JUST BEHIND THE CHAMBER, ARE PORTRAITS OF EVERY FORMER SPEAKER SINCE FREDERICK A. C. MUHLENBERG, ELECTED IN 1789. THE COLLECTION WAS BEGUN FORMALLY IN 1910, AND INCLUDES A JOHN SINGER SARGENT PORTRAIT OF THOMAS BRACKETT REED. THE CARPET WAS WOVEN TO HARMONIZE WITH THE MINTON TILES OF THE ADJACENT RETIRING ROOMS.

responsive to the people's will. Indeed, popular election of senators only began with the ratification of the Seventeenth Amendment in 1913; until that time the House was the only forum that represented the people directly. It is fitting, therefore, that among its specific functions is responsibility for originating all revenue bills, for this is a matter that from the beginning was thought to be best kept close to the people. The House also has the power to impeach federal officers, a power it exercised when it voted to impeach President Andrew Johnson in 1868 and came close to exercising again against Richard Nixon in 1974.

The House of Representatives had as its model the House of Commons, the lower house of the British Parliament, and many of its customs and procedures derive from that body. Both houses have a Speaker who presides over the chamber, but whereas the British official is essentially a parliamentary functionary—an impartial moderator of debate—the role of his American counterpart has evolved into a far more powerful one. This is largely the legacy of Henry Clay, who was elected Speaker on his first day in the House. Never content in a passive role, Clay used the office to further the interests of both his party and his region. Subsequent Speakers have followed his lead; the holder of the office today wields enormous political power, in addition to being second, after the vice president, in line of succession to the Presidency.

While trying to get his party's legislative program passed, the Speaker must also fulfill his historic function of controlling the proceedings on the floor. For this he appoints a parliamentarian, whose job it is to see that proper parliamentary procedures are followed. These, too, are based on British models and are designed to ensure that passions be kept under control and that all voices be heard. What strikes the modern ear as excessive formality is simply a way to keep the debate among so many Members focused on the issues, and to prevent it from degenerating into personal attack. Members seldom refer to one another by name; personal relationships are sublimated into "my distinguished colleague," or "the distinguished gentleman" or "gentlewoman."

Such rules of debate and procedure generally succeed in preserving the decorum of the House, although there have been incidents of beatings and canings, and even the occasional hurled inkwell. If necessary, the Sergeant at Arms will move about the floor "presenting" the mace —the symbol of legislative authority—which he brings into the chamber whenever the House meets.

The 1970s brought two important technological innovations to the House Chamber. In 1973 a sophisticated electronic voting system was installed to expedite what had become a time-consuming process. To record their votes, Members now insert identification cards into machines located in every other row of seats. The tally is recorded on the gallery walls, which are transformed into screens when a vote is being taken. A lighted display at either end of the chamber shows the resolution under consideration, the current tabulation of votes, and the time remaining.

Even more revolutionary was the House's decision in 1979 to allow television coverage of floor proceedings. Television had been tried in the House as early as 1947, but had been adamantly opposed by Speaker Sam Rayburn, who feared it would cheapen the conduct of government and encourage posturing and flamboyance among Members. Supporters of television coverage argued that it would bring the legislative process to the American people, allowing millions to "sit in the gallery." It would also enable Members to keep abreast of what was going on when they could not be in the chamber. The intense interest generated by coverage of the Watergate hearings in 1973, and the subsequent committee sessions on the impeachment of President Nixon, helped to overcome any lingering resistance: In 1979 the House of Representatives began gavel-to-gavel coverage of its deliberations. The Cable Satellite Public Affairs Network (C-SPAN) in turn broadcasts this coverage to cable subscribers nationwide. At the end of each day, after the House has completed its regular business, Members may request up to one hour of time to speak—to an empty chamber and millions of viewers—on any subject they wish.

Joint sessions of Congress fulfill a constitutional duty and are held in the House Chamber because of its larger size. The Constitution requires the President to "give to the Congress Information of the State of the Union." Jefferson, however, thought the idea of the President appearing before Congress smacked of the king addressing Parliament, and since he was also an indifferent public speaker, he began the tradition of delivering the "Annual Message" in writing. Since Woodrow Wilson, however, most Presidents have given their State of the Union addresses in person before a joint session, and in 1965 Lyndon Johnson began the custom of an evening session so that it could be televised live to a broader audience. On these occasions, the Speaker of the House and the president of the Senate preside together, and Members are joined by

the Supreme Court, the Cabinet, senior military officials, and representatives from the diplomatic corps. During the Cold War era there was concern about having the top officials of all three branches of the federal government so publicly assembled in one place, and since then one Cabinet member has always remained absent, but which one that shall be, how chosen, or where he or she is secreted in the interim, are closely guarded secrets.

A joint session is also held every four years in order to count the electoral ballots for the Presidency, and whenever else the situation warrants it. On April 2, 1917, Woodrow Wilson asked Congress to declare war on Germany; a year and a half later he had the happier task of reporting peace. On December 8, 1941, Franklin Roosevelt spoke of the Japanese attack on Pearl Harbor, "a date which will live in infamy." On September 11, 1990, George Bush told a joint session that Iraq had invaded Kuwait; on March 6, 1991, he announced the liberation of Kuwait.

The House and Senate come together for ceremonial reasons in joint meetings, and to be invited to address one of these is among the highest honors the nation has to offer. On April 19, 1951, General Douglas MacArthur, in announcing his retirement, recalled for Congress the refrain of a ballad: "Old soldiers never die; they just fade away." Astronauts have been warmly welcomed to the podium. Kings, queens, emperors, presidents, and a shah have all stood before the Speaker's desk. In November 1989, Lech Walesa, the leader of the Polish labor union Solidarity, was interrupted repeatedly by applause as he insisted that he was still an electrician, only pretending to be a diplomat. He voiced his appreciation for the words of encouragement he had heard, but noted that "the supply of words on the world market is plentiful," and asked for his country not charity, not philanthropy, but rather cooperation under decent and favorable conditions. A few months later the playwright president of Czechoslovakia, Vaclav Hável, gave eloquent voice to the aspirations of his newly liberated country: "A person who cannot move and lead a somewhat normal life because he is pinned under a boulder has more time to think about his hopes than someone who is not trapped that way." And then came Nelson Mandela, freed after twenty-seven years in jail, who struck an unassailable chord with his American audience: "We could not have known of your Declaration of Independence and not elected to join in the struggle to guarantee the people's life, liberty and the pursuit of happiness. . . ." One of the most enthusiastic welcomes ever extended by Congress to a foreign leader was in June 1992 for Boris Yeltsin, the first popularly elected President of Russia in its more than one-thousand-year history. Yeltsin declared that the idol of Communism had collapsed, never to rise again, and vowed that "there will be no more lies—ever."

FACING PAGE: A PORTRAIT OF GEORGE WASHINGTON WAS COMMISSIONED IN 1832—THE CENTENNIAL OF HIS BIRTH—AS A COMPANION PIECE TO ONE OF GENERAL LAFAYETTE; SINCE 1834 THE TWO PORTRAITS HAVE ALWAYS HUNG IN THE HOUSE CHAMBER. JOHN VANDERLYN, WHO PAINTED WASHINGTON, WAS TOLD TO COPY THE HEAD FROM THE WELL-KNOWN LANSDOWNE PORTRAIT PAINTED BY HIS OWN TEACHER, GILBERT STUART. ABOVE, IN THE GALLERY, MAY BE SEEN PART OF THE ELECTRONIC VOTING SYSTEM; ON THE BACK OF THE CHAIR IN THE FOREGROUND IS ONE OF THE MACHINES MEMBERS USE TO RECORD THEIR VOTES.

THE SENATE:
WHERE PASSIONS
ARE COOLED

ON January 4, 1859, the senators marched in solemn procession from the old chamber into their new one. It had greatly expanded gallery space, and the acoustics were more than adequate. A cast-iron ceiling with ornamental glass skylights, similar to that in the House, would cause trouble later on, and the room lacked the intimate elegance of the old room, Still, at its unveiling it received generally favorable notices. Like their colleagues in the House, senators had cloakrooms just outside the chamber and a retiring room behind it—the Marble Room—one of the most lavish examples of Thomas U. Walter's work in the Capitol.

⌁ Tragically, as had been the case in 1810, events were again conspiring to deny some senators much time to enjoy their new home. In less than two years South Carolina voted to secede from the Union, moving the country inexorably toward civil war. In January 1861, Jefferson Davis took his own leave of the Senate in one of the most poignant speeches ever delivered on that floor: "I am sure I feel no hostility toward you, Senators from the North. I am sure there is not one of you, whatever sharp discussion there may have been between us, to whom I cannot now say, in the presence of my God, I wish you well; and such, I am sure, is the feeling of the people whom I

𝒜 BUST OF JOHN ADAMS, THE
FIRST VICE PRESIDENT, BY
DANIEL CHESTER FRENCH—
PART OF THE VICE PRESIDEN-
TIAL COLLECTION IN THE GAL-
LERY OF THE SENATE CHAMBER.
FACING PAGE: THE ROSTRUM IN
THE SENATE CHAMBER.

represent towards those whom you represent. I therefore feel that I but express their desire when I say I hope, and they hope for, peaceable relations with you, though we must part."

Within months the Capitol was occupied by recruits of the Sixth Massachusetts Regiment, one of whom, far from reciprocating Davis's benevolent sentiments, sought out his desk in the chamber, intent on destroying it with his bayonet. He was caught in the act by Isaac Bassett, the assistant doorkeeper, who insisted that the desk belonged not to Jefferson Davis but to the Government of the United States. The repaired desk is still in use; a wooden inlay marks the spot where the bayonet struck.

The Senate Chamber was remodeled between 1949 and 1951. As in the House, the ornate but unsafe ceiling was replaced with one of steel and plaster, and a much-improved air-conditioning system eliminated the need for Congress to adjourn each spring because of the heat. Unlike the House, however, the Senate Chamber contains many reminders of its history. Sixty-four of the mahogany desks had been used in the Old Senate Chamber; the earliest ones were purchased in 1819, and as states joined the Union, exact copies were added. Beginning in the 1830s, three-inch-high mahogany writing boxes were added to them, to provide more space for senators whose entire office space usually consisted of their desks. Only Daniel Webster refused to allow his to be changed, insisting that what had been good enough for his predecessors was good enough for him. Today his desk remains the way he wanted it, and is always assigned to the senior senator from New Hampshire.

The desks are arranged with a central aisle dividing the two parties. By custom, Democrats, as the older party, sit to the right of the Presiding Officer, and Republicans to the left. Only once in the nation's history, in 1881, was the Senate evenly divided between Democrats and Republicans.

On ledges on either side of the rostrum are lacquered snuffboxes. Although rarely used now, they are kept filled, a reminder of a time when the habit was so common that vice president Millard Fillmore complained that too many senators milling around the snuffboxes prevented him from hearing the proceedings. Henry Clay is said to have visited the snuffboxes as a diversion when speeches became tiresome. Another relic are the spittoons; few now chew tobacco, but they are there if needed.

The appearance of the Senate Chamber can be described as sober. Apart from the collection of vice presidential busts in the gallery niches, there is little in the way of art. Mottoes surmount the central doors on three walls: *Annuit Coeptis* ("God has favored our undertakings"), *Novus Ordo Seclorum* ("A new order of the ages is born"), and *In God We Trust*. Below them are marble panels representing Patriotism,

FACING PAGE: THE CORRIDOR LEADING TO THE EAST DOORWAY INTO THE SENATE CHAMBER. THE FLOOR AND THE COLUMNS ARE MARBLE; THE WALLS ARE SCAGLIOLA, AN IMITATION MARBLE MADE OF POLISHED GYPSUM THAT WAS USED THROUGHOUT THE EXTENSIONS. THE CORINTHIAN CAPITALS FEATURE, IN ADDITION TO THE ACANTHUS LEAF, UNIQUELY AMERICAN ELEMENTS: CORN, TOBACCO, AND MAGNOLIA FLOWERS AND LEAVES. *PAGES 176-77:* THE SENATE CHAMBER DURING A VOTE ON THE CONSTITUTIONAL AMENDMENT TO BALANCE THE BUDGET, JUNE 30, 1992. MATTERS OF GRAVE IMPORTANCE MAY BE DEBATED AND VOTED ON BY THE FULL SENATE IN THE CHAMBER. MORE TYPICALLY, SENATORS COME AND GO DURING DEBATES, OR SIMPLY MILL ABOUT WITH THEIR COLLEAGUES WHILE WAITING TO VOTE. SENATORS SPEAK FROM THEIR OWN DESKS; WHEN READY TO DO SO, ONE OF THE PAGES SITTING AT THE FOOT OF THE ROSTRUM HURRIES OVER WITH A PORTABLE LECTERN, AND A STENOTYPE REPORTER MOVES NEAR ENOUGH TO MAKE A VERBATIM RECORD FOR THE *CONGRESSIONAL RECORD*. THE LEGISLATIVE CLERK SITS WITH THE PARLIAMENTARIAN AT THE MARBLE DESK IN FRONT OF THE PRESIDING OFFICER, AND CALLS THE ROLL TO RECORD VOTES.

Courage, and Wisdom. Above the rostrum is the national motto, *E Pluribus Unum*. The Senate Chamber is all business.

The room befits what is the most powerful upper house of any legislative body in the world. The framers of the Constitution had a useful model for the House of Representatives in the British House of Commons, but the House of Lords was nothing they wished to emulate. Instead, the Senate was patterned after the upper houses of several state legislatures. Its role is spelled out "with exquisite imprecision" in the Constitution, which states only that each state shall have equal representation in it, that it shall have the power to try impeachments, and that it shall give advice and consent to the President on treaties and nominations. The hope and expectation was that it would be above partisan and parochial concerns—a voice of reason, deliberation, and accommodation. George Washington is said to have described it as the saucer into which the passions of the nation should be poured to cool.

Until 1913, senators were elected by their state legislatures. The system worked well during the early nineteenth century, but as political parties grew stronger it resulted in frequent deadlocks, especially when the upper and lower houses of those legislatures were controlled by different parties. Some Senate seats went unfilled for years; for anyone truly desperate to win one, the opportunities for bribery were rampant. Amid complaints that the Senate was becoming a millionaires' club, proposals for reform were regularly passed in the House—and just as regularly rejected by the Senate. In 1911, the spirit of the progressive era finally reached the Senate; it passed the Seventeenth Amendment to the Constitution, providing for the direct election of senators. The amendment went into effect on May 31, 1913, but its immediate impact was nil; every incumbent senator was reelected in 1914. It was, however, a landmark in the expansion of representative democracy.

The major difference between the Senate and the House is size: one hundred senators versus 435 representatives. Senators enjoy the luxury of time, representatives need to hurry along. Strict rules govern how long representatives may speak, and on what subject. Rules of the Senate not only allow virtually unlimited debate, but actually encourage it "among those who need no encouragement." Such latitude sometimes appears to allow matters to move unnecessarily slowly, but as President Truman remarked: "Whenever you have an efficient government, you have a dictatorship." The House may debate a matter for a day or two, while the Senate may devote weeks to the same subject.

One aspect of the unlimited time rule is the filibuster—a time-honored device peculiar to the Senate and first employed as early as 1789. On March 2, 1917, two days before the end of the second session of the Sixty-fourth Congress, President Wilson's request for authority to arm American merchant ships against overt German submarine activity reached the Senate. When a small number of isolationists succeeded in blocking the bill by talking until the session ended, the outraged President railed against a system in which a "little group of willful men, representing no opinion but their own, have rendered the great government of the United States helpless and contemptible." He, and the nation, demanded an end to such paralyzing abuses. A few days later, in a special session, the Senate's first cloture rule was overwhelmingly approved.

The rule was not intended to eliminate filibusters, and during the twentieth century new records for verbosity have been established. In 1935 the flamboyant Huey P. Long spoke to an amused gallery for more than fifteen hours, including in his remarks instructions on the best way to fry oysters and his own recipe for "potlikker." Strom Thurmond holds the record for the longest single filibuster speech: twenty-four hours and eighteen minutes in opposition to the Civil Rights Act of 1957. The cloture rule has undergone modifications since 1917, but filibusters remain accepted Senate practice.

The House has the power to impeach federal officials, and the Senate then tries the case, either to acquit or remove. The most famous trial, in 1868, was that of President Andrew Johnson, who was accused of violating the Tenure of Office Act and conspiring against Congress and the Constitution. In an unprecedented spectacle the Senate acquitted Johnson by the margin of a single vote.

The Senate also consents to the ratification of treaties, and none was more bitterly divisive than the Treaty of Versailles at the end of World War I, with its provisions for establishing the League of Nations. President Wilson had proposed the League as an instrument for maintaining international peace, and had succeeded, with some difficulty, in securing support for it at Versailles. He misjudged the Senate, however, in thinking ratification at home would be quick and automatic. Opponents feared it would mean surrendering the nation's autonomy, and on March 19, 1920, when the final vote was taken in the Senate, it failed to win the necessary two-thirds majority. The United States signed a separate peace treaty with Germany in 1921 and never joined the League of Nations.

Another constitutional power of the Senate is to confirm Presidential appointments. After passing initial committee scrutiny, a nomination goes to the chamber for debate and a vote by the full Senate. Much of this now takes place before the critical eye of the television camera. Senators resisted the introduction of television longer than their colleagues

Daniel Webster's desk in the Senate chamber. Senators keep their desks for the entire length of their term; as they move up in seniority their desks usually move with them—toward the center front of the chamber. The desks have nameplates, and when the decision was made in the late nineteenth century to omit "Mr." from the senators' names, the conscientious assistant doorkeeper, Mr. Bassett, bemoaned the "great liberty, amounting to profanation, [that had] been taken with senatorial dignity." Senatorial dignity has not, however, prevented graffiti; many senators write or carve their names inside the desks they occupy.

in the House. Among other things, they feared that their unlimited time rule could too easily be abused by self-promoters. A trial period showed that the advantages outweighed the disadvantages, however, and since 1986 television cameras have recorded events in the Senate Chamber.

Minor issues or procedural matters are sometimes handled by voice votes, but on all important matters voting is still done the old-fashioned way, with the legislative clerk calling the roll and recording the *yea*s and *nay*s. A system of bells summons senators to the chamber to vote—the only time they are required to be present. To ensure attendance, bells used to be installed in the favorite Capitol Hill watering holes, but the advent of electronic pagers has made them unnecessary. After the first bell, senators are allowed fifteen minutes to get to the chamber floor; fortunately for them, even the most outlying offices are connected with the Capitol by subway. What began in 1909 with yellow battery-powered Studebaker buses is now a fast and efficient system. It would be hard to improve upon the reverential sentiments expressed by the Chaplain of the Senate at the official opening ceremony:

> . . . these swift chariots of democracy . . . defying distance in their swift transit, bear as their cargo the hopes and fears, the problems and purposes of the whole world. . . . The concerns of untold millions will be riding on these wheels as across the hours of each day they swing to and fro like a weaver's shuttle, helping to fashion the fabric of the Nation's welfare.

And should the weaver's shuttle not swing quite quickly enough, the Doorkeeper has been known to "readjust" the hands of the official clock with a broom handle.

FROM THE BEGINNING, the Capitol has been built with the same faith and optimism that built the country. George Washington expressed it when he asked in his Farewell Address: "Is there a doubt whether a common government can embrace so large a sphere?" and then answered his own question: "It is well worth a fair and full experiment." As the infant nation struggled into existence, he laid the cornerstone of the building that was to be the home of its government. Two hundred years later both the country and its Capitol have grown in ways unforeseeable then, and yet they both embody the same hopes and principles that led to their birth. The country is still engaged in the experiment in democracy—a system that Theodore Roosevelt called both the noblest and the most difficult of all forms of government and that Winston Churchill called "the worst . . . devised by the wit of man, except for all the others." And the Capitol is still the home and the symbol of that experiment.

FACING PAGE: THE LUXURIOUS MARBLE ROOM IS RESERVED FOR THE EXCLUSIVE USE OF SENATORS—A PLACE WHERE THEY CAN READ AND RELAX AND STILL BE JUST A FEW STEPS FROM THE CHAMBER. EVERYTHING IN THE ROOM, EXCEPT THE FLOOR, IS MARBLE: WHITE ITALIAN MARBLE FOR THE CEILING, PILASTERS, AND CORINTHIAN COLUMNS, AND BROWN VARIEGATED TENNESSEE MARBLE FOR THE WALLS. IT IS HARD TO VISUALIZE TROOPS BEDDING DOWN HERE, OR BACON HANGING FROM THE CEILING—BOTH OF WHICH WERE SAID TO HAVE HAPPENED DURING THE CIVIL WAR.

A WINDOW IN THE SENATE
LIBRARY FRAMES THE MALL,
THE WASHINGTON MONUMENT,
AND THE LINCOLN MEMORIAL.
ACROSS THE POTOMAC IS
ARLINGTON CEMETERY, WHERE
LIES PIERRE L'ENFANT, THE
DIFFICULT AND UNCOMPROMIS-
ING VISIONARY WHO WROTE:
"NO NATION, PERHAPS, HAD
EVER BEFORE THE OPPORTU-
NITY OFFERED THEM OF DELIB-
ERATELY DECIDING ON THE
SPOT WHERE THEIR CAPITAL
CITY SHOULD BE FIXED. . . .
AND ALTHOUGH THE MEANS
NOW WITHIN THE POWER OF
THE COUNTRY ARE NOT SUCH
AS TO PURSUE THE DESIGN TO
ANY GREAT EXTENT IT WILL
BE OBVIOUS THAT THE PLAN
SHOULD BE DRAWN ON SUCH A
SCALE AS TO LEAVE ROOM FOR
THE AGGRANDIZEMENT AND
EMBELLISHMENT WHICH THE
INCREASE OF THE WEALTH OF
THE NATION WILL PERMIT IT
TO PURSUE AT ANY PERIOD,
HOWEVER REMOTE." TO LOOK
IN ANY DIRECTION FROM THE
CAPITOL IS TO SEE HOW BRIL-
LIANTLY L'ENFANT ACHIEVED
HIS "MAIN OBJECT."

ACKNOWLEDGMENTS

This book began with meetings, first with Walter J. Stewart, Secretary of the Senate, and then with members of the United States Capitol Preservation Commission. With their co-operation and approval, we were given the freedom to interpret the United States Capitol as it appears in these pages. I especially wish to acknowledge Tom Gonzales, General Counsel to the Secretary of the Senate, who lent every assistance possible to make the book's production proceed smoothly and successfully. Thanks are also due to George White, Architect of the Capitol, and to the Capitol architectural historians, Barbara Wolanin and Bill Allen, for their knowledgeable involvement in this book. Jim Ketchum, Senate Curator of Art, was not only a friend, but was invaluable for his scholarly assistance, from inception to completion, in the work we did in the grand rooms that are his responsibility. His associates, Scott Strong, John B. Odell, and Richard L. Doerner, were equally tireless and unfailingly cheerful during our marathon photographic sessions. Many thanks are also due to those keepers of the gate who were responsible for our having the necessary signed permits so we could work: Bob Bean, Pat McNally, Sergeant John Krug, Bob Cooksey, Caroline Klemp, Ellsworth Jackson, and Maurice Johnson. I am indebted to John Mullenholz for his time and wise counsel at critical stages, and to my agent, Audrey Wolf, for her optimism, encouragement, and perseverance. Many thanks are due to Edward H. Fowler, Jr., R.W., Grand Master of Masons in Pennsylvania, for his involvement and generosity. I could not possibly have accomplished my work without a small army of available photographic assistants; these loyal troupers were often with me from before dawn until late into the night. John Wiltse and Carl Caruso were my model lighting technicians; along with Grant Russell and Rick Roth, they were responsible for maneuvering and setting up cartloads of equipment and for reading the mind of a sometimes overly demanding and generally impossible boss. Also helping out when their schedules permitted were Martin LePire, Howard Connelly, Michael Jones, Ben Smith, Kathy Janoski, Andy Sohn, and Sophia, Marc, and Paul Maroon. I am especially indebted to Eastman Kodak Professional Photography division for generously supplying the film and processing for this book. My lighting inside the Capitol was affected by the warm color quality of the lights in the chandeliers and also by the color palette of the walls, which needed to be cooled down in order to balance with my color film. Kodak patiently advised and worked with me until I arrived at the proper combination of compensation gels necessary. Dick Baghdassarian, of Pro Photo, skillfully devised and constructed a multi-lens holder for the gelatin filters I needed for the different lenses I used. The Ektachrome was processed at Chrome, Inc., and the Kodachrome through Pro Photo, both of Washington. All film was 35mm, and the Leica R system was used throughout, with lenses ranging from 15mm to 180mm, and with 1.4× and 2× extenders when necessary. I used quartz lights with Photoflex umbrellas. Much appreciation is due to Chuck Hyman, whose expert eyes not only recognize perfect color, but also the components necessary to achieve it.

A million thanks to the people at Stewart, Tabori & Chang for their beautiful bookmaking—especially to Maureen Graney and Ann ffolliott for their professional attention to those countless details that refine and define a book. Many thanks to Jim Wageman for his inspired design, and to his associate, Howard Johnson, as well as to Barbara Sturman for her typesetting and Hope Koturo for her care in production. In closing, my heartfelt gratitude to my wife and co-author in all things, Suzy. —FRED J. MAROON

I could never have undertaken this book without the comforting assurance that some of the most knowledgeable people on Capitol Hill would be looking over my shoulder as I went along. Richard A. Baker and Raymond W. Smock, the Senate and House Historians, Donald A. Ritchie, Associate Historian of the Senate, and Cynthia Miller, Assistant Historian of the House, shared with me their wealth of knowledge about the building and its occupants. Barbara Wolanin, Curator in the Office of the Architect of the Capitol, came up with answers to all my questions and provided me every access to the resources in her office. And Jim Ketchum—what can I say but that every author should have the support of such a sage and encouraging presence! All of these read through my text, and were generous with their time and constructive with their comments. I am particularly indebted to Bill Allen, Architectural Historian in the Office of the Architect, for giving me the benefit of his vast knowledge about his "favorite subject," for his patient and meticulous reading of what I had written, and his unfailing good humor. Tom Gonzales also deserves my thanks for supporting this book and its authors from start to finish. I will be forever grateful to David Howell, Constantine Roussos, and Mark Taylor, who helped restore my sanity and my hard disk when both were in imminent danger of crashing. Without them this might have been a very short book. Among the many who answered questions for me, cleared up confusions, dug up needed documentation, and made helpful suggestions were Charles Atherton and Roger Haley. Ann ffolliott, at Stewart, Tabori & Chang, was all I could ever want in an editor: erudite, discerning, diplomatic, and calm—even when she had every reason not to be. And last but never least, my thanks to my husband, Fred, for his unwavering confidence and encouragement. —SUZY MAROON

BIBLIOGRAPHY

Allen, William C. *The United States Capitol: A Brief Architectural History.* Washington, D.C.: U.S. Government Printing Office, 1990.

Allen, William C. *The Dome of the United States Capitol: An Architectural History.* Washington, D.C.: U.S. Government Printing Office, 1992.

Arnebeck, Robert. *Through a Fiery Trial: Building Washington 1790-1800.* Lanham, Md.: Madison Books, 1991.

Art in the United States Capitol. Washington, D.C.: U.S. Government Printing Office, 1978.

Bowling, Kenneth R. *Creating the Federal City, 1774-1800: Potomac Fever.* Washington, D.C.: The American Institute of Architects Press, 1988.

Brown, Glenn. *History of the U.S. Capitol.* 2 vols. Washington, D.C.: U.S. Government Printing Office, 1900-1903.

Bryan, Wilhelmus Bogart. *A History of the National Capital.* New York: Macmillan, 1916.

Byrd, Robert C. *The Senate, 1789-1989.* Vols. 1 and 2. Washington, D.C.: U.S. Government Printing Office, 1988.

Caemmerer, H. Paul. *The Life of Pierre Charles L'Enfant.* Washington, D.C.: National Republic Publishing Company, 1950.

The Capitol. Ninth edition. Washington, D.C.: U.S. Government Printing Office, 1988.

Congress A–Z. Washington, D.C.: Congressional Quarterly, Inc., 1988.

The District of Columbia. New York: Time-Life Books, 1968.

Dole, Bob. *Historical Almanac of the 19th Century Senate.* Washington, D.C.: U.S. Government Printing Office, 1989.

Durbin, Louise. *Inaugural Cavalcade.* New York: Dodd, Mead & Co., 1971.

Fairman, Charles E. *Art and Artists of the U. S. Capitol.* Washington, D.C.: U.S. Government Printing Office, 1927.

Fogle, Jeanne. *Two Hundred Years.* Arlington, Va.: Vandamere Press, 1991.

Frary, Ihna Thayer. *They Built the Capitol.* Richmond: Garrett and Massie, 1940.

Girouard, Mark. *Cities and People.* New Haven: Yale University Press, 1985.

Green, Constance McLaughlin. *Washington.* Princeton: Princeton University Press, 1962.

Highsmith, Carol M. and Ted Landphair. *Pennsylvania Avenue: America's Main Street.* Washington, D.C.: American Institute of Architects Press, 1988.

Hutson, James H. *To Make All Laws: The Congress of the United States, 1789-1989.* Washington, D.C.: Library of Congress, 1989.

Josephy, Alvin M., Jr. *History of the Congress of the United States.* New York: American Heritage Publishing Company, 1975.

Josephy, Alvin M., Jr. *On the Hill.* New York: Simon & Schuster, 1975.

Kite, Elizabeth. *L'Enfant and Washington, 1791-1792.* Baltimore: Johns Hopkins Press, 1929.

Latimer, Louise Payson. *Your Washington and Mine.* New York: Charles Scribner's Sons, 1924.

Miller, Lillian B. *Patrons and Patriotism.* Chicago and London: University of Chicago Press, 1966.

Smith, A. Robert with Eric Sevareid and Fred J. Maroon. *Washington: Magnificent Capital.* Garden City, N.Y.: Doubleday & Company, 1965.

Smith, Steven S. and Christopher J. Deering. *Committees in Congress.* Washington, D.C.: Congressional Quarterly Press, 1990.

Thomas Jefferson and the National Capital. Edited by Saul K. Padover. Washington, D.C.: U.S. Government Printing Office, 1946.

We, the People. Washington, D.C.: United States Capitol Historical Society, in cooperation with the National Geographic Society, 1991.

Designed by Jim Wageman

Layout assistance by
Howard Johnson

Composed in Minion
with QuarkXPress 3.1
on a Macintosh IISI by
Barbara Sturman,
Stewart, Tabori & Chang,
New York, New York

Color separations by
Professional Graphics,
Inc., Rockford, Illinois

Printed by
Northeast Graphics,
North Haven,
Connecticut

Bound by
Horowitz/Rae Book
Manufacturers,
Inc., Fairfield,
New Jersey